Quarterly Essay 53: That Sinking Feeling

Asylum Seekers And The Search For The Indonesian Solution

Paul Toohey

16

EasyRead Large

RHYW

Copyright Page from the Original Book

Quarterly Essay is published four times a year by Black Inc., an imprint of Schwartz Media Pty Ltd. Publisher: Morry Schwartz.

ISBN 978-1-86395-646-8 ISSN 1832-0953

Subscriptions – 1 year (4 issues): $59 within Australia incl. GST. Outside Australia $89.
2 years (8 issues): $105 within Australia incl. GST. Outside Australia $165.

Payment may be made by Mastercard or Visa, or by cheque made out to Schwartz Media. Payment includes postage and handling.

To subscribe, fill out and post the subscription card or form inside this issue, or subscribe online:

www.quarterlyessay.com
subscribe@blackincbooks.com
Phone: 61 3 9486 0288

Correspondence should be addressed to:

The Editor, Quarterly Essay
37–39 Langridge Street
Collingwood VIC 3066 Australia
Phone: 61 3 9486 0288 / Fax: 61 3 9486 0244
Email: quarterlyessay@blackincbooks.com

Editor: Chris Feik. Management: Sophy Williams, Caitlin Yates. Publicity: Elisabeth Young. Design: Guy Mirabella. Assistant Editor/Production Coordinator: Nikola Lusk. Typesetting: Duncan Blachford.

Printed by Griffin Press, Australia. The paper used to produce this book comes from wood grown in sustainable forests.

THAT SINKING FEELING

Asylum Seekers and the Search for the Indonesian Solution

Paul Toohey

ALI REZA AND THE TWENTY ASYLUM SEEKERS

All the frustration and hatred Ali Reza Bahrami had ever known welled within him and spilled forth. It was directed at a group of Iranian asylum seekers, all of them men, all of them in the final stages of preparation to catch a boat from Indonesia to Australia. Reza was walking in angry circles, punching his chest, defining himself, standing his ground, poking his finger sharply into Iranian chests. He was just one young man, aged twenty-three, and an Afghan. He was badly outnumbered in terms of ethnicity and physical size, but he refused to back down.

We felt some responsibility for Reza, who had been acting as our informal translator and guide in the small mountaintop city of Cisarua, in central West Java, the place where most of the asylum seekers wanting to get to Australia come to find a smuggler and passage south. Reza was digging himself deeper, abusing the Iranians in their own Farsi language, one of the many in which he was fluent. Some of the Iranians were kissing him on the face, telling him to calm down. Others looked menacing. I got the feeling Reza was about to be stabbed. Our appeals for Reza to get control of himself were under assault from his own rising fury, as he screamed that he would never again, under any circumstance, explain himself to an Iranian.

After two years of living in Cisarua, and three in Malaysia before that, Reza knew the local asylum scene intimately – who was passenger or smuggler, old hand or recent arrival. Reza had brought us up a steep narrow road to a villa, occupied by twenty or more Iranian men. We were in a smuggler's villa and ought not have been there. We had asked Reza if he knew a group that was ready to sail. He said he did and had brought us straight here. He had earlier befriended one of the members of this group, who were now on standby, ready to shift at a moment's notice in mini-vans or trucks down to the southern coast and onto a smuggler's boat.

In only one sense was this group any different to the other small groups of mostly Afghans and Iranians who openly wandered this hilltop town, bored, using the internet cafés, window shopping the things they'd seen many times before, buying nothing but essentials because they would need their money further down the line, hopefully in Australia. These Iranians were quarantined, meaning no contact with any outsiders. They were tour packaged for Christmas Island, ready to sail. It was Friday 20 July 2013. Initially, with Reza translating, everything had gone well.

The conversation was very different to what it would have been in this same city in late 2007, when Kevin Rudd, as the new prime minister, ordered Manus Island and Nauru to close on humanitarian grounds and ended the temporary protection visa program.[1] Back then it was difficult to get anyone in Cisarua to admit they were trying to take a boat. They would swear they were there to register with the United Nations High Commissioner for Refugees (UNHCR), to gain formal status as refugees, and ideally to have their accommodation and a living stipend paid by the International Organization for Migration (IOM) as they awaited orderly resettlement in a First World country – which they prayed would be Australia. Some of them, particularly the single mothers with clutches of children, said they were prepared to wait for years, if that's what it took, in the hope of resettlement – even though they had just a one in ten chance of getting one of the 80,000 annual global resettlement places on offer. But most were there for the boats.

1 Temporary protection visas required holders to reapply for a second TPV after three years, with the prospect of being sent home if home conditions were deemed improved. holders were also denied access to family reunion pro-grams and barred from returning to Australia should they leave for any reason.

Rudd could afford the luxury of a conscience, then, because he had arrived in office to find the Manus and Nauru offshore facilities all but empty, and it was deemed that temporary protection visas were too harsh. There were no boats, apart from the odd freak vessel. By general agreement, John Howard, assisted by a lull in international people flows, had stopped them.

Rudd's shift soon aroused interest in South Asia – the countries from Afghanistan down to Sri Lanka – and the Middle East, in places such as Quetta, Kabul, Kandahar, Tehran and Abadan City, home to high numbers of discontented and at-risk people. Some of these began to move down to Indonesia again. At first, most were Afghan Hazaras and Sri Lankan Tamils, who were coming to the losing end of a 26-year civil war. There were also people from Burma's Muslim Rohingya minority, though they were scattered and disorganised, more downtrodden and less able to raise the smugglers' fees. Slower to move, initially, were the Iranians, although they would soon begin to gather in great numbers.

They entered Indonesia in various ways. Most, excepting the Iranians, could not turn up at Jakarta's Soekarno-Hatta International Airport and apply for visas-on-arrival. The Sri Lankans would set sail east across the Indian Ocean for Malaysia, or the westernmost Indonesian island of Sumatra, where they would find smugglers to ferry and bus them to the central West Java province of Bogor, where Cisarua is located. Those coming from the neighbourhoods of Afghanistan and Pakistan would fly to Malaysia, which issued visas-on-arrival to most nationalities, and catch inter-island ferries to Indonesia. These were usually the smaller groups, who were not as yet in the hands of smugglers or their agents. But they typically had the name and number of someone who could help, or had plans to meet some of their own people in Indonesia and gain introduction to a smuggler. Others, particularly the Iranians, had been flying directly to Jakarta as half-disguised tour groups, sometimes with an agent on the same flight herding them through. That was until Indonesia banned on-the-spot visas for Iranians in mid-2013, supposedly in response to a personal request from Rudd to President Susilo Bambang Yudhoyono (so it was reported in Australia, but later, when things went bad during the spying scandal, senior Indonesian ministers would say they'd cut the visa-on-arrival program not to help Australia, but because too many Iranians were bringing drug problems to Indonesia).

Sri Lankans liked to avoid attention and were hustled down to Bogor to disappear into their own networks, lying low. Most of the other groups moved more openly. Upon arrival in Jakarta, they would book into one of several usual-suspect hotels, where they would meet their smuggler and do business. It was important to asylum seekers that they did this face-to-face, preferably with someone from their own country or ethnicity.

People shopped with smugglers who had a reputation for getting people to Christmas Island safely. Death-boat smugglers went out of business, or kept operations going by hiding in the shadows behind lieutenants. Not only were passengers investing what might amount to their earthly wealth, they were often travelling with children and wanted assurances the boats were safe. They also wanted to know that they would not be arrested in Indonesia. Such guarantees were easily given. These customer – smuggler meetings showed how intimate the operations were. After the asylum trade restarted in early 2008, the Australian Federal Police in Jakarta would come to the view that there were not really any smuggling Mr Bigs, not in the sense of snakehead triad bosses or masterminds hiding behind complex walls of front companies. They were small-time businessmen crooks, usually from Iraq, Iran or Afghanistan, living openly in Jakarta and growing rich on the proceeds of smuggling.

The smuggler bosses often used Arabic pseudonyms, such as Abu Wasim or Abu Yunis (Abu means "father of" and is as meaningless as calling someone "Mister"). These men declared themselves to be Hajji, meaning they had made the pilgrimage to Mecca. It gave them an element of credibility with their Muslim clients, they wrongly imagined, because Hajji were expected to be honest men. The passengers were not so naive as to place store in the Hajji deceit, and they would later laugh ruefully about it when boats sank or their money went missing.

Assistance was also provided so passengers could access their money to pay for the trip. This was not always as straightforward as making multiple withdrawals from a cash machine, especially for Iranians, whose banks were subject to UN sanctions and non-operational in Indonesia. The Iranians usually paid $5000 to $8000 for boat passage to Christmas Island, which did not include their flights to Jakarta. They made arrangements with trusted relatives back home to shift money to the smugglers' bank accounts once a family group had safely made it to Indonesia. Or the smugglers would introduce them to local moneychangers, who would charge high transaction fees to change cash bundles to US dollars, the only currency the smugglers accepted. The business deals were conducted with solemn grace, the smugglers listening sadly to their customers' tales, assuring them as they counted their money that the struggle was almost over.

The Afghan asylum seekers got a better deal, being historically the steadiest customers. Not only did they travel slightly cheaper, apparently for the simple reason that they were poorer, but they were also not expected to stump up cash before travel. Trusted relatives would only transfer money to the smugglers upon news of a confirmed landfall on Christmas Island (where new arrivals had the right to make a short call, anywhere in the world, to tell relatives they were safe). The Afghans paid for success. The Iranians had been using the Cisarua route since the time of *Tampa,* but the black market took a different view of them to the Afghans. Between 2010 and 2013, the Iranians had become especially impatient customers. They required rapid passage to Australia, with no dawdling in Indonesia. Under such terms, the smugglers were able to demand higher fees and strict cash upfront.

Passengers would make their way down to Cisarua, ninety minutes south of Jakarta, a trip which could quickly turn into four hours in heavy traffic, where they would move in with friends, occupy accommodation provided by the IOM, or be met by the smugglers' agent, typically Iraqi, Iranian, Afghan or Sri Lankan, who would act as guardian for the new passengers, shovelling them into short-term accommodation. These same agents would also be monitoring the streets, on constant lookout for straggler groups that needed a boat. Whoever the asylum seeker was, however they had come, they almost always ended up in this resort city.

Cisarua is set amid active volcanoes and tea plantations, and home to a sizeable prostitute population. There were white-skinned Moroccan women, who catered to wealthy Indonesian clients, and Indonesian women, who tended to come from other regions in order to protect local Sundanese sensibilities, catering to Arabic vacationers. Security men working the hotel carparks were the first contact for the hookers, who did not walk the streets but were available by request. Everything in Cisarua was in your face, yet behind the thinnest screen. Some of the city's signage was Indonesian and Arabic, not indicative of a community lean towards sharia law as might be seen in Aceh, but in deference to the large number of Saudis and Kuwaitis who came to visit the Taman Safari game park, to take mountain treks and four-wheel-drive expeditions, or to idle in villas where the strictures of home were relaxed. One young Saudi diplomat told me his dad owned a villa in Cisarua. Asked why they were so attached to the place, he said: "It's cheap and it rains every afternoon." Young men in shorts and thongs brought their black-burqa brides for honeymoons, gathering in the cool and clean local Pizza Hut, where the women lifted their cloth muzzles to sip Coke through straws and eat. With only their heavily painted eyes visible behind the slits, they seemed loaded with intriguing sexuality. (Note to self for future thesis: *Is the burqa failing to achieve its intended purpose?)* Many more groups of young Saudi men came without women, partying with girls-for-hire and alcohol behind the high-walled villas. Or so the local hotel security men claimed. Wealthy Chinese-Indonesians filled the sprawling cliffside hotels on weekends.

At a glance, the Arabic influence seemed due to the asylum seekers, with shops in the bazaar selling hookahs, pistachios, dates and oranges. But it was actually an effect of the longstanding Saudi and Kuwaiti visitors, who kept a careful distance from the asylum seekers, regarding them as an unseemly presence in their holiday town. Off the main road, the place is a collection of private villas: some luxurious, some mid-range, some scummed-out and past their prime, the tennis courts showing weeds in the earthquake cracks. Local landlords unable to afford upgrades had gladly turned over their faded resort properties to the asylum seekers who were there for the long haul, rent guaranteed by the IOM. Or they provided short-stay deals, cramming up to fifty passengers into a single dwelling while the smugglers waited for boats to become available.

Those villas that were loaded with imminent travellers were badly kept local secrets, as were the villas where the local smuggler bosses lived – often with Indonesian wives and kids, which showed how comfortably settled they were in this town. One night I witnessed some fifty asylum seekers raid the villa of their smuggler, demanding their money back after he and his agents had repeatedly failed to make good on their promise that the group was to sail the following day. Punches were thrown and there was a mini-riot in the smuggler's front yard, set in a heavily populated alley. No neighbour called the police. Or if they did, the police did not come. Cisarua, on any day post-2008, was brimming with asylum seekers, smugglers and the wealthy, casually dressed Saudis, who did not appreciate being mistaken by a journalist for Australia-bound desperados.

Registering with the UNHCR was a formality for many asylum seekers, even if they had every intention of catching a boat. Once settled in Cisarua, they would take the two-hour train ride north back to central Jakarta and queue, sometimes for days, outside the UNHCR building in the Sabang area, entering not through the main entrance but by a small rear laneway. There they milled about, waiting for appointments. After being granted an interview, they would get a one-page slip of paper called a UN Refugee Certificate. Their names would enter circulation as people who needed a new country, and the long wait would begin.

Even though Indonesia is not a signatory to the UN convention on refugees, it tolerates the UN's presence. The UN, and the IOM, which is tasked with trying to persuade people to return home, brought some small sense of order to the 10,000–15,000 asylum seekers, and many more registered refugees, who were at any time in Java, hoping for resettlement or a boat. Having a Refugee Certificate was the first official step to a new life, but it did not mean they were formally acknowledged as refugees. It only meant the process had begun. The real benefit of holding this black and white photocopied document was to keep police off their backs. No asylum seeker or refugee who was in Indonesia for more than a few months wanted to move around in public without having this document in their wallet or handbag.

Yet no one ever deregistered with the UNHCR when they snuck off to catch a boat. Now, five years on from Rudd's policy shift, there were at least thirty Persian smuggling agents living in Cisarua, offering passage south on questionable vessels. That was beside the Sri Lankan, Afghan and Arab specialist smugglers.

The group of Iranians surrounding Reza in the smuggler's compound had not bothered with the UNHCR procedures – they'd been moving too fast. They had left Iran only ten days earlier. The 2013 Australian federal election was looming and any pretense of waiting for legal resettlement had been abandoned. So many boats had been leaving, transporting more than 25,000 by sea in the past twelve months, and approaching 50,000 since Rudd had softened asylum policy, that no one any longer bothered denying their plans. They were taking the boats.

"Of course," they said.

LEGAL OR ILLEGAL, A BOAT IS A BOAT

Downstream, Australia had been having a long argument with itself over use of the term "illegals" to describe asylum seekers. The pro-asylum network – different to the pro-refugee "network," being those who favoured orderly resettlement of registered refugees (Philip Ruddock always considered himself pro-refugee) – had more or less won this debate. They said everyone had a legal right to seek asylum, therefore ought not be described as illegal. The government, the Opposition and the media, who'd been counselled by the Australian Press Council on this point, generally played along, avoiding its use. But sometimes it just slipped out. If you were a journalist, this would lead to a hasty email rebuke from Marilyn Shepherd, an asylum campaigner whose Google Alerts, presumably set to trawl for the terms "asylum seeker," "refugee," "Indonesia" and "illegals," flashed up when stories went online after midnight. "You fools..." she would write in messages that were sent out around 3 or 4a.m. as she stalked the pre-dawn news world, hunting stupid journalists.

The asylum cause had never owned any part of Julia Gillard's heart, and Rudd's had conveniently gone missing. The asylum network had badly needed a win of some sort, and while the illegals debate had permitted celebration of a rare victory, the party was held in the smallest self-circulating echelons. It was also a uniquely Australian semantic indulgence. The debate was never going to shift public opinion, and advanced no real cause. Who had really thought of the boat arrivals as *legals?* Most had entered Indonesia illegally; and doing business with the smugglers was hardly above board, given that running people-smuggling operations was now illegal in Indonesia. Moreover, Indonesian crews were being locked up in Australian prisons for the criminal offence of bringing people, who were supposedly not "illegals," on boats. No Indonesian crew member ever mounted a convincing legal defence, to my knowledge, that they were conducting a philanthropic exercise. Some lawyers claimed their clients had no knowledge they were taking people to Australia, having been told they were going on fishing expeditions, or believing Christmas Island was part of Indonesia. That, speaking Australian, was bullshit.

Then came a startling finding: the passengers were illegal, after all. This was courtesy of the ABC's newly raised Fact Check unit, which delivered its verdict just before the 7 September 2013 election. It tested the Opposition immigration spokesman Scott Morrison's use of the term "illegal entry" for people arriving by boat. The unit had investigated an inquiry from citizens who presumably expected and hoped the ABC would censure Morrison. Fact Check consulted two former solicitors-general and relevant refugee academics. It decreed that Morrison was correct: "Based on the definition set out in the United Nations people smuggling protocol, people who have come to Australia without a valid visa have illegally entered the country," the unit decided. "That is the case even though these people have not committed any crime, nor broken any Australian or international law." And the 1951 Refugee Convention also referred to people making "illegal entry."

This side battle would not be worth mentioning but for the intimation that accompanied the complaint: that smugglers provided a lawful humanitarian service. It was not something pro-asylum advocates said too loudly, because there had been too many dead people at sea, and there were about to be more. But it was there. In a lecture on the asylum crisis given in Melbourne, in March 2012, refugee activist Peter Farago declared himself a "former people smuggler," and told of sneaking people out of Hungary to escape the Nazis. On many levels, the analogy did not work, the least of which being that Farago did not shift people for personal gain, nor did he set them up for failure by shipping them out on ruined boats with inadequate safety equipment. Most telling, he would have faced execution if caught. Even setting aside the substantial problem of linking Indonesia or the upstream asylum-source countries to Nazi Germany, to align himself with the contemporary people smugglers seemed a careless abdication of his own proud story.

Yet, at times, I had considered the idea of smugglers as merely providers of a service. After all, it was the passengers who created the demand for boats, even if the smugglers ran doorway travel agencies in places such as Quetta, offering seductive family deals, all children travelling free. An author, Robin de Crespigny, had written a book that told the tale of a compassionate Iraqi smuggler, Ali Al Jenabi, who turned to shifting people by boat to Australia because he was sickened by the exploitative ways of Java's smugglers. But had Al Jenabi put people on a boat that sank or capsized, there would have been no book. It was when you saw certain things you'd never forget – such as a Sri Lankan mother screaming as she held her small dead son, pulled from the water off the south coast of Java, or images shot on smartphones of an asylum boat heaving and hammering into the vicious cliffs of Christmas Island, in December 2010, killing fifty people or more – that these arguments foundered.

Chris Evans, immigration minister under Rudd, and Chris Bowen, immigration minister for most of Julia Gillard's term, attempted to alter the nature of the public discourse by getting asylum-sympathetic Labor voters to look at the problem in a different way. John Howard's government had gone after both passengers and smugglers. The Labor ministers tried to avert eyes from the growing number of arriving boats by targeting people smugglers as the direct cause of the misery. This skirted the fact that so many asylum seekers knew the risks and were prepared to take them; that they were in on the deal, though often at the unhappy end of it. Ultimately, the argument went beyond worthless sophistry because the smugglers did not provide a quality service. They were ruthless. They had killed hundreds. Expressions of remorse did not stand out as memorable arguments-in-mitigation for the handful of smugglers sentenced in Australian or Indonesian courts.

I would learn that distaste for the smugglers existed in a place I did not expect to find it: among those refugees stuck in Cisarua, awaiting formal First World resettlement with the UNHCR, with no intention of ever catching a boat. They viewed the smugglers as the most immediate reason for their long delay in getting to Australia, because every time another group of hopefuls turned up in Indonesia, and every time another boat shipped out, there was a chance that those who made it to Christmas Island would be counted in Australia's capped annual humanitarian intake (which under Labor was, initially, 13,750), thereby denying them a place. They were equally angry with the UNHCR for taking so long to process their cases, meaning some would lose hope and eventually send forth family envoys – usually, the father or eldest son – on boats. The UNHCR could not find them places in Australia because the places had been taken. What these asylum seekers were complaining about, even though they did not use the term, a Philip Ruddock-era relic (and Bob Hawke before him), were queue jumpers.

Long after Ruddock, the Refugee Council of Australia, in an online information section called "Myths about refugees and asylum seekers," acknowledged the existence of queue jumping, in a way: "The myth that asylum seekers take places away from refugees who are resettled from overseas does have some basis in truth. However, this is not because asylum seekers are trying to rort the system or 'jump the queue' – they have a right to seek asylum and Australia has a legal and moral obligation to process their claims. Rather, it is the direct result of Australian Government policy."

That seemed more or less right. No one was trying consciously to "jump the queue." They were just coming. Governments pulled their annual quota of humanitarian applicants from refugee camps and trouble spots around the globe, in preference to those who arrived on boats. However, boat arrivals were being counted in the annual humanitarian intake; almost half of them. Before Rudd's reinstatement of tough policy in mid-2013, those who could afford to take the boats *were* taking the place of people who were not only waiting in refugee camps, but also in the unofficial refugee camp that was Indonesia's Cisarua.

And no one hated smugglers – especially Iranian smugglers – quite like Reza, who had been waiting five years with his mother and siblings for legal resettlement, having seen thousands arrive in Cisarua and succeed in forcing their way through to new lives in Australia on the boats. He was quite clear that he did not resent anyone who made it all the way to Christmas Island on a boat; he wished them well. He despised the facilitators who had ensured that his family, with its longstanding claim, kept being pushed to the back of what could only be called, from his perspective, a queue.

"Give me two weeks with your police and I can show you every smuggler in Cisarua," Reza told me. I had no doubt he could. We had asked him if he could show us a smuggler's villa, and he'd taken us directly to one. But back where he'd come from, as an Afghan living in Iran, prosecutions were built on the basis of prejudice, not evidence. The Australian Federal Police in Jakarta were not able to conduct independent investigations in Indonesia, because they had no legal standing in a foreign land. I presumed the AFP had sources in Cisarua, providing information in return for favourable consideration of their refugee claims. If so, this information was not translating to results when it was passed on to their Indonesian counterparts. Clearly, the Indonesians lacked the interest, will and resources to investigate or disrupt the rampant smuggling industry. Their tolerance of the situation in Cisarua, and the uninterrupted boat movement off the coast of southern Java, was evidence of that. The smugglers and the passengers were out there to go and grab, if so desired. But most of the arrests came after a boat had gone down and angry survivors, with no chance of getting their money back, started pointing the finger and naming their smugglers.

In the villa, the Iranians were calm as Reza translated the news that on the previous day, 19 July, Rudd had unveiled his Papua New Guinea Solution. Rudd was capable of many surprises, but this would stand as the most self-serving and rankly chameleon of his interrupted prime-ministership. People would, from this moment, be processed in PNG and could, if found to be refugees, settle into a new life in Port Moresby. Or Mount Hagan. Or Lae. Or some other malarial swamp that was the cultural antithesis of everything they knew. Or they could go to some other country that would take them. But not Australia.

The Iranians had not heard about this. Some of them could read English, even if they could not speak it well. I passed my iPhone, showing them the opening sentence of Rudd's media release: "As of today asylum seekers who come here by boat without a visa will never be settled in Australia." It was the least ambiguous statement issued in six years of Labor rule. It read like the work of a quality tabloid backbench subeditor. No matter which way you read or re-read it, crunched it, inverted it or tried to peek around its corners, it said exactly the same thing. One Iranian man studied the text and turned to the others to translate it. Together, they ran a quick analysis. The words should have shocked them, but no one seemed upset. They didn't believe it. This policy adjustment, they believed, did not affect them.

Any Australian reading the same sentence would have been entitled to doubt Rudd's sincerity, because he had earned Australia's doubt. Whatever he said was subject to revision, should expedience require it. The Iranians, with only headline knowledge of our politics, had arrived at the same conclusion, though from a different place. They did not believe Rudd's heart was in the statement. They said, sharply: "Australia is a kind country." They raised their chins and added, in rebuke-challenge: "You are kind people."

I would encounter such rhetorical assurance-seeking many times from asylum seekers in Java. It did not seem honest to leave their delusions untroubled. They had become – setting aside the carbon tax – the biggest political issue in Australia, and they deserved to hear it. They were not welcome, not if they came by boat. You could see in their clouded faces that they didn't get it, or didn't want to get it. They did not see themselves as invaders, but valued additions. They believed Australia cared about them, that we wanted them to come. They regarded us as a compassionate people who welcomed all comers, however they got to Australia. This was not just spin fed to them by their smugglers. They had evidence to support their view: many had family and friends who had already made it under Rudd and Julia Gillard. They also knew people who had made it under John Howard. They knew the hurdles, the time possibly lost in camps while their claims were sorted. But these were mere intermissions. Mister Kevin Rudd, as they called him, would not say no.

They were less sure about Mister Tony Abbott, who the headlines were predicting would have an easy win in the 2013 election. The Iranians came from a place void of political shade, where leadership thrived on internal menace and outward confrontation. Australia was not such a place, yet Mister Abbott was saying he'd stop the boats, by turning them back if needed. They were not sure what to make of this. In Australia, anyone who looked beyond Abbott's slogan had to wonder whether he would be true to his word. Unless Abbott got a firm deal with Indonesia to take back the boats, he was inviting trouble. It would involve Australia's military physically forcing humans back toward Indonesian shores. Furthermore, if people refused to turn around, and scuttled their boats, and people died, Abbott would have a problem not only at home, but with the world.

Abbott said an incoming Coalition government had no intention of violating Indonesian sovereignty, just as he would not expect Indonesia to violate ours. The clear inference was that he expected Indonesia to act unilaterally to stop the boats, and the clear complaint was that it had been violating Australian sovereignty for more than a decade by letting boats sail south from Java, and all points east and west on the archipelago. The Iranians were not acquainted with the way that the Australia v. Southeast Asia push-and-shove always settled down, usually after a large cash incentive from Australia concealed under the title of some AusAID program; nor did they understand that this time Abbott was playing a dangerous game with Indonesia that a cash apology might not settle. But their instincts about him were right. That was why the rush was on.

Labor's foreign minister, Bob Carr, had come out recently to say that most of the people coming by boat were economic migrants, meaning their claims of persecution were not genuine. There was no question he was referring to Iranians, such as the sharp-dressed people in shining white no-brand sportswear we were sitting with in the smuggler's villa. The number of Iranians began slowly surging across 2011 and 2012, even though Afghans were still the biggest cohort coming by boat during that period. But from June 2012 to June 2013, the (financial) year when 25,126 people came by boat, assisted by 667 Indonesian crew, Sri Lankans led the numbers with 6862 boat arrivals, followed by 6579 Iranians. And these Iranians had come out of nowhere, suddenly and easily overtaking the Hazaras, most of whom could readily prove they were suffering persecution, whether they'd come directly from Afghanistan or were living as exiles in Iran or in Pakistan – where, in the city of Quetta, there was a program afoot to suicide-bomb them from the face of the earth.

Though Sri Lankans had become the biggest cohort, Australians – if I was not wrong – had some sense that they were running from real trouble. We kind of *got* Sri Lankans. There was more concern about the emerging Iranian – aka Muslim – arrivals. Yet sifting through the ethnicities, nationalities and backgrounds of the boat people (another term that occasionally slipped out) was not an Australian pastime. As the boat push to Australia began strongly informing debate in the long 2013 federal election lead-up, just as it had back in 2001, the Iranians, Afghans and Iraqis were seen as one generic Muslim morass. They were Arabs, most probably. Where we saw no difference, there were chasms. We really didn't want to know.

Some of the "true" Iranians, who were definitely not Arab but Persian, feared the time was coming when fathers, sons and possibly even daughters would be conscripted to fight for the Syrian government; some had involvement in dissident political groups, or had converted to Christianity. But the Iranians I spoke to had not even bothered wording themselves up with stories of religious or political persecution that they might run past ASIO once they disembarked on Christmas Island. They said they wanted to leave their country and start again in a free country with better jobs. As they took their journeys, they certainly saw themselves as illegals, at some level: hiding out in villas, preparing to run the soft gauntlet down to the coast past the opportunely sleepy military, police or naval posts, leaving on dawn boats, was no normal travel itinerary.

The other core group of asylum-seeking Iranians had most likely come from Iran's Khuzestan Province, along the Iraq border, at the top of the Persian Gulf. They were tribal Arabs, who had occupied the region for millennia or had crossed from Iraq into Iran in the time of Saddam Hussein and settled into border cities such as Abadan and Ahwaz. Many had pioneered the journey in the time of *Tampa,* and now those left behind were catching up, because they'd had enough and the time was right. They felt themselves unwelcome Arabs trapped in Persian Iran. Persians considered them lazy and recalcitrant, and potentially Iraqi allies. The Arab Iranians considered themselves to be at the end of the queue for education and employment in Iran, and first in line for ethnic-based mistreatment.

This group more clearly fit the UN's refugee criteria, each being a person who "owing to well-founded fear of being persecuted for reasons of race, religion, nationality, membership of a particular social group or political opinion, is outside the country of his nationality and is unable or, owing to such fear, is unwilling to avail himself of the protection of that country; or who, not having a nationality and being outside the country of his former habitual residence as a result of such events, is unable or, owing to such fear, is unwilling to return to it." The Persian Iranians, Bob Carr's economic refugees, mostly did not. That is why they did not bother applying for a UN Refugee Certificate in Jakarta. It took too long to stand in line to get one, and they would likely have failed the interviews anyway. They would also struggle to win Australia's protection if and when they made it to Christmas Island by boat. But they were trying anyway. If it all went wrong, there was a chance they could return to Iran and resume life. They were always in a hurry, and not only because there was a potential change of government in Australia. If their journey for any reason failed and ended in Indonesia, they could be back home in a matter of weeks: their government would assume they'd just taken a holiday.

The Right, for want of a better term, and which on this point included Carr, viewed anyone who had not done the long haul in a refugee camp or was not in possession of a valid UN Refugee Certificate as likely to fit the category of economic refugee. The opposing view was that no one's motives should be damned before they had a chance to apply for Australia's protection; and that the UN definition did not preclude a person with money from being classed a refugee. And even if you were a genuinely persecuted person, you were denied the opportunity to make a living. Everyone was, at some level, an economic refugee.

The freedom-seeking, "cashed-up" Persian Iranians, Carr's economic refugees, saw themselves living a bellowing daily tragedy under the totalitarian mullahs. If life was passably survivable, it did not follow that it was acceptable or tolerable. That was why they were leaving. These Iranians were skilled. Economic migrant *was* more or less the correct term for many of them, even if Bob Carr knew there was a deeper story as to their reasons for flight. But it was not one he was going to delve into with an election on the way. The Arab Iranians liked to show you collages on YouTube of their people being hanged in public places. The Persians may have been a few steps further from the noose, but that didn't mean they liked life in Iran.

Everything about the Persian Iranians suggested their political inclination was deep-seated conservatism. They were self-starting small-business people who would one day likely make solid Coalition voters, if they made it. The Cubans who fled to Florida in two main tranches became instant Republicans, for the obvious reason that they were fleeing communism. The Latinos crossing by land into the United States were typically Democrat in their early days, because that's where they sensed the welcoming sympathies lay; although that was subject to change as they became more settled and accepted. Australia's Aborigines, sometimes likened to internally displaced people, had in the north after long decades of blind Labor allegiance begun to turn from Labor, as they sought more effective political support. Carr was right about the economic refugees, but there was an untellable appendix to what he was saying: so what?

From the time of the Vietnamese boat people with their alleged gold bars, we condemned wealthy arrivals because they would take the place of the poor arrivals.

Yet we had little sympathy for the poor arrivals. There was a seething national antipathy towards unlawful maritime arrivals, even if the Greens leader, Christine Milne, claimed that the "overwhelming majority" of Australians supported more compassion for asylum seekers. You had to think she had an especially small circle of drinking buddies. Summarising national sentiment was hazardous, but as a starting point you could look to Bob Hawke's 1989 statement on asylum seekers fleeing Cambodia: "Do not let any people, or any group of people in the world, think that because Australia has that proud record, that all they've got to do is break the rules, jump the queue, lob here and Bob's your uncle, other than in accordance with the appropriate rules. Bob is not your uncle on this issue." Then there was the 2001 election result. Howard was likely going to lose that election until *Tampa* sailed in, with 438 asylum seekers, to save his neck. No major-party politician had ever dared campaign on a policy of warmth and understanding towards people coming on boats. The ABC's Vote Compass, launched on the day Rudd called the 2013 election, produced the biggest online survey in Australian history with an effective sample size of 570,000 respondents. It found that 40 per cent of Labor voters agreed with Rudd's policy that no one who arrived by boat should ever be permitted to settle in Australia. Polling research was telling Labor what it already knew: there was little sympathy for asylum seekers among its voter base. Vote Compass found the further you got away from the inner cities, the more the sympathy evaporated.

For now, the Iranians liked Labor, because Rudd had given them the opportunity to come, even if that meant coming by boat. They did not translate Rudd's betrayal of asylum seekers in his reclamation of the leadership as something that could possibly affect them. But it did. Directly. The incoming policies of the outgoing Rudd were more hardcore than the longstanding policies of the Coalition, which had never varied its views from the time of Howard's "[W]e will decide who comes to this country and the circumstances in which they come." This statement, once portrayed as the most damning evidence of Howard's small-mindedness, now looked slightly quaint in the rear-vision mirror. Rudd had set an IED under his own Dietrich Bonhoeffer monograph, published in the *Monthly* in 2006, the year before his election, in which he argued that Bonhoeffer's compassionate Christianity was not antithetical to modern governance. Rudd was the Good Samaritan on asylum seekers. "The biblical injunction to care for the stranger in our midst is clear," wrote Rudd. Now, seven years on, Rudd was, to borrow one of his own terms, rat-fucking asylum seekers to win himself another term.

As a reporter, you could make the asylum story work by reporting it straight. If you told the tragic story of a drowned boat kid, the Right interpreted it as the cruelty of the people-smuggling trade. The Left said it was evidence of the cruelty of Australia in denying them a place. It was win-win reporting, if you stuck to the story. The warring opinion writers – who tended not to acquaint themselves with individual people or cases, perhaps recognising that actually meeting someone who came off a boat might give rise to inconvenient nuances (sympathy, repulsion) – took their respective readers to two outskirts at either end of town, where the characters were victims or villains. It must have been an easy thing to wake each morning knowing you were set on a path that never varied between black and white, right and wrong, good and bad, your only task to re-enlighten your devoted reader and hopefully make them slightly more angry or anxious than they were yesterday. The asylum seekers of Java were not one thing. Some were cunning; some were desperate. Some had false hopes of quick acceptance in Australia; some well knew the difficulties that awaited them upon arrival; some viewed us as the hardest country to get to; some saw us as the easiest. Some were rolling the dice, having a go; others felt they had no choice. When it went wrong, as they lay shocked, wet and trembling in the aftermath of disaster, beaten by the unworkable equation of bad boats on high seas, you could see them for what they really were: weary, weary people.

WAITING FOR AUSTRALIA

Sitting with a group of Afghan women in an IOM-funded villa in Cisarua, a fifteen-year-old Afghan boy was throwing his clothes into a suitcase in the middle of the room. He had Australian flags stitched on a pair of jeans that were going into his bag. With Reza translating, I asked the young man: "Are you going to catch a boat?" He replied: "Yes. I will catch a boat." I suggested that Ardiles Rante, the photographer I was working with, take some shots: it seemed newsworthy, a young man preparing to head south, in spite of Rudd's decree. Reza advised me in a quiet aside that the young man was actually not off to catch a boat; he was putting on a performance for the benefit of his mother. He was threatening to move out, because they were arguing about his girlfriend. The women in the room were mostly single mothers who would never take the boats. Nor would they ever go back to Afghanistan, or to the places where they had lived as outsiders, in Iran or Pakistan. Over tea served in glass cups, the women were asking about Australia. That was the nature of so many interviews – they would reverse into interrogations. They wanted to know about jobs, the cost of living and their level of acceptance, as Muslims, should they make it. I told them that the greatest freedom Australia offered was the freedom not to believe in God. We'd more or less got rid of him; he was not required. One woman buried her face in her hands, appalled. They all looked slightly alarmed. But this was one bit of useful information I could provide. Their acceptance in Australia, if they made it and were not to disappear into strict cultural enclaves, would require them first to accept *us.* Then one of the women said something that started them all laughing. Maybe it didn't seem such a bad idea, living somewhere godless.

Yet getting too close to asylum seekers could be soul-destroying. With those stuck in Indonesia, awaiting UNHCR approval, or stranded after being robbed by the smugglers, every interview would finish with the same words: "Can you help me?" They would ask that you approach the Australian government, or the UNHCR or IOM, on their behalf. What could you do but promise to write a story? Even that was a convenient lie. It was not possible to tell all their stories. Yet they were remarkably unselfish, never trying to steal you away to write only their family's story, but dragging in all the neighbours so they could also bear witness. In the end, you had to extricate yourself, with excuses.

Some had lost hope altogether and were stuck, no longer knowing what to do. In Cisarua, I met one family of ethnic Tajiks from Afghanistan, a group rarely seen in Indonesia. They had lost two rounds of appeals to the UNHCR to be recognised as refugees; and no one got more than two attempts. The IOM had given them notice that it would stop paying their accommodation within a few weeks. Abdul Basir

Bashardost, aged forty-seven, had paid money to the smugglers in 2011 to take his wife and five children to Australia, but they were ripped off and lost everything.

Bashardost, when applying for refugee status for his family, made the mistake of telling the UNCHR what was very likely a true story: that he had worked for the Afghan government's intelligence service in pre-Taliban times, under Mohammad Najibullah Ahmadzai, aka Najib, the last of the Soviet-backed Afghan presidents. Najib was ousted in 1992, and castrated and publicly hanged by the Taliban in 1996. Bashardost said the UNHCR suspected he may have been involved in torturing prisoners under the Najib regime. Despised by both Taliban hardliners and the current government, the family fled to Quetta, in Pakistan, where he said he faced revenge threats from people who knew something of his past.

"We have no answers," he said. "They say [we can't go to Australia because] we are Tajik, not Hazara. I can't return to Afghanistan." He said an arrest warrant was issued in Afghanistan in 2004. And Pakistan would not accept them back, now that the UNHCR had rejected them. Bashardost, a heavy-set man, would sit on the porch of his villa, staring off into nowhere. He would try to smile for the sake of his family, but it came out broken and hopeless; he felt a crushing guilt for his personal history, which had now dragged his wife and children – who came into his life long after he had worked in intelligence – into an impossible situation. His wife, Nabila, aged thirty-six, was a striking woman: so many faces in one, seeming to speak of the entire antecedents of the Caucasian people. She spoke no English, but the eldest daughter, Sanggita, aged fifteen, did. Sanggita was an especially hard person to meet; she had so much life, strength and intelligence, and so little hope to go on with. She kept up the spirits of her four younger siblings and her parents. She made no excuses for her father's past, whatever it was. She spoke the English she had learned on her asylum travels rapidly and fluently, demanding to know what was to become of her siblings, Samerar, Tarina, Samim and the youngest in the family, Sajjid, aged six. None of the children had been to school since the time they arrived in Cisarua in 2011. All the kids did all day was play with other asylum-seeker kids. Everyone else, in this particular compound of villas, loved them. But because their father had told the truth, he had condemned his family. If Sanggita was sometimes shrill, I could understand it. There was no solution for her family. I could not give her the answers she wanted, but these people came from places where the line between media and government was confused. They seemed to think we were one and the same. At such times, you wished it were true – that you could hook them directly into your government. But you never did that. Though I soon would break the rule, on one occasion, and it would not prove a successful intervention.

***

One of the Iranians studied the PM's words on my smartphone. He handed the phone back. "I'm not going to PNG," he said.

"You won't have a choice," I told him.

They didn't believe the Rudd statement because they couldn't afford to believe it. The men explained they had already paid $8000, each, for their passage. They were going. Maybe tonight. A young fit man wearing an athletic singlet and a gold chain called Reza over. They began arguing and pushing. The language was foreign, but the message was clear: why have you brought a journalist and a photographer to my villa? This guy, an Iranian, was a local organiser, a fixer, working for someone bigger. His job was to stay here, in Cisarua, collecting groups of Iranians, keeping them together, waiting for word of when the boat was ready to depart. Part of his job was to remove the mobile phones from the asylum seekers, in case they were fifth columnists prepared to pass on their location to the authorities as they moved to the coast. There were no televisions or radios in the villa, which assisted in keeping the prospective passengers in an information void, so they didn't get to hear about things that could distract them from their ambition, such as the Rudd announcement. Most likely this cog in the smuggler network was not only making good money off the passengers; when the time came, he would receive free passage south, to throw himself on the mercy of Australia too.

The Iranian agent dialled a number and handed the phone to Reza, who now found himself talking directly to the organiser, a Farsi speaker based in Jakarta, who was berating him for revealing the location of the villa. Reza was holding the phone at arm's length, screaming back at the smuggler boss. People were circling; they were now taking the smuggler boss's view that Reza had imperilled their boat journey. I was getting nervous. I told Reza it was time to leave.

"I need ten more minutes with these fucking arseholes," Reza said.

"You haven't got ten minutes," I told him. He wasn't listening.

Reza had spent five years in Malaysia and Indonesia, trying to get to Australia. And now he was so close. He'd been accepted for legal resettlement in New Zealand, but he didn't want New Zealand. For all asylum seekers who made it to Indonesia, there was only one place: Australia. Reza's girlfriend, an asylum seeker he'd fallen in love with in Indonesia, had in the previous week won legal resettlement in Australia. She was in Brisbane. She'd made it. He was desperate to be with her.

Drawing New Zealand as your new home in the UNHCR resettlement program was better than being in Iran, Afghanistan, Pakistan, Malaysia or Indonesia, but still a crushing disappointment. If so many New Zealanders didn't want to live in New Zealand, why would anyone else? The Burmese Rohingya and the

Sri Lankans saw some hope in New Zealand, but less so the Iranians, Iraqis and Afghans. All their networks were in Australia. Being accepted by New Zealand was, to their mind, another interruption on the way to their destination. They knew people in Australia. They had friends there. They Facebooked, emailed, texted and phoned them. And now the prime minister had announced that Australia was out of bounds. You could chance your life on the boats, but you'd never settle.

Only PNG would give you a home, if you could bear it. From the cradle of civilisation to its still-savage outskirts, living alongside blacks in a crime-ridden, part-Christian, part-animist hellhole, with one mosque in the whole country? Rudd understood the joke very well. So did PNG's prime minister, Peter O'Neill. Acceptance of Rudd's deal contained implicit humiliation for O'Neill, like the audience member who volunteers for the hypnotist's stage. No one – maybe a handful of asylum seekers at most – would ever choose to live in O'Neill's beautifully rotten country. He played along well, doing good business, accepting Rudd's deal by taking Australian money for health and universities.

Reza and his family had evaded Rudd's PNG Solution and were going to New Zealand, in a few weeks. It was just a matter of arranging departure dates. For him now to get stabbed or beaten for sake of his Afghan pride would be pointless, but he didn't care. Attempts to pull him physically from the scene and shove him in the car worked only for a moment. He jumped straight back out, going straight for the smuggler's agent, and they began wrestling across the yard. As they screamed at each other, Reza turned to me and said: "These men are not refugees, they are rich, they are going on a holiday." I just wanted to get him out of there.

We struck a deal: Reza's deal. He said he would leave only on the condition we parked the car outside the villa gates, so he could walk away, by himself, without being seen to be in the protection or company of this Australian journalist, because it would diminish him as an Afghan. You could see how these people had been able to see off centuries of attempts at invasion: theirs was the purest tempered and forged pride on this earth. He gave his word to me as an Afghan – albeit one who had never been to Afghanistan – that he would leave. So we waited outside the gates. With one more flurry of outrage, Reza left and took his seat in the car. He was not even breathing hard.

"What the hell was that all about, Reza?"

"I fucking hate Iranians," he said. "I will never ever again take orders from an Iranian."

Later, back at his accommodation a young woman with the sharpest, darkest eyebrows came out of Reza's brother's bedroom. I asked her where she was from. Iran. "I don't hate all Iranians," Reza explained. "Just some Iranians."

Reza and his mother, Soghra Ahmadi, told the story of how they had come to Cisarua. Soghra, now forty, had left Kabul in Afghanistan and crossed to Iran when she was aged six. "There was fighting," she explained. "I was young. I no understand." From that time, Reza's family had been kicked around at the bottom end of Iranian society. The family never had proper papers and constantly feared being deported to Afghanistan. Reza, born twenty-three years ago in Mashhad, in Khorasan Province, was very bright but always an outsider, and denied a tertiary education unless he took up religious studies, which he refused to do. He despised the Iranians for treating him as a second-class person. He would never forgive them for refusing him, as a person born in Iran, the right to better himself. And for treating his mother, Soghra, as a serf.

Reza's father had taken a smuggler's boat to Europe, years earlier. "He went to Europe to start a new life," Reza said. "He was never seen again." Reza's father may have drowned at sea, but perhaps not. His parents had not only suffered at the hands of the Pashtun majority in Afghanistan, and for being a minority in Iran, they had inherited a further problem: their own Hazara intra-clan dispute. Soghra, at the age of thirteen, had been betrothed to a man twenty years older than her in a deal it was hoped would bring two warring clans, now both living in Iran, together. Soghra and her groom had met for the first time on their wedding day. At the age of fourteen she'd had her first child. The marriage didn't work. Reza said his mother and father never loved each other, that it was possible his dad made it to freedom in Europe and never looked back.

Reza had come to Malaysia with his mother and two brothers five years ago, where they registered with the UNHCR as refugees. They investigated taking a boat to Australia but did not have the money and Soghra considered it too dangerous. Malaysia was a revelation. They were free to work and quick-minded Reza was able to avoid trouble with the authorities. He spent three years working under a Chinese tailor, the UNHCR employed him for his language skills, and he worked in a restaurant. He was making money, but resettlement was coming too slowly. In 2011 they took a Pakistani smuggler's boat to Cisarua, having heard the UNHCR was resettling people faster in Indonesia. The family members were forbidden to work and it was impossible to get on with life while waiting. Soghra earned small money selling flatbread; Reza went stir-crazy. It had been a long wait, but now they were going to New Zealand.

Soghra, removing her headscarf, explained the first thing she planned to do upon arrival. "I will throw this away," she said.

DOWN MEXICO WAY

No Australian government permitted the public to hear the true thoughts of its diggers, air force or navy while they were engaged in warfare or operations. It could not risk a serviceperson saying something stupid or thoughtless about the enemy, such as they'd like to blow them to pieces, or, even worse, expressing misgivings about progress. The ventilation of such views might lead to more problematic questions on the depth of political commitment to any given mission. The statements of our suited and uniformed leaders showed great discipline and total divorce from reality.

No one could doubt the depth of Senator John Faulkner's feelings when he, as defence minister, was required to announce and grieve yet another soldier killed in Afghanistan. You could see he really did feel personal responsibility, as the responsible minister; you could see it in his heavy steps to the podium and in his frustrated sadness. Faulkner claimed to support the war. He had to. But who really believed him? There was invariably a widow nearby, who didn't want to believe her partner's death was in vain; he had to think of her.

The ordinary Australian soldier did not talk to the media, except when playing staged dusty cricket games in a warzone on Boxing Day, or accepting medals for under-explained actions. The frontline people working the northern waters under Border Protection Command, who were also encouraged to think of themselves as participants in a war, never talked under any circumstance, unless as witnesses in coronial investigations. Every Australian serviceperson was constrained to silence, permitting politicians to lay claim to their unquestioning support.

Our American allies did not understand this. Their view on free speech was informed by their founding document, the Constitution, which has been called a "paradox of secular revelation" because it does not mention God, yet is regarded as divine. The US serviceperson was permitted to support, resent or question their particular war or security effort, and to speak about it. They had earned the entitlement: it was they, not the politicians, who were out there fighting. Despite being given the adult responsibility of handling both a gun and a voice, US servicepeople did not tend to run down their country. They were simply more informative and interesting than their Australian counterparts, whether on military or humanitarian deployments. What this meant, in practical terms, was that if you wanted to know what was going on, go ask an American.

The policy of openness existed down on the border between the US and Mexico, where people crossed north, in numbers, over the miserable wastelands every day. Down Mexico way, authorities never described the Mexicans or those who came from further south as economic refugees or economic migrants. Such terms were redundant because they were all economic migrants. No one called them asylum seekers. They were all illegals.

In 2011, in the Brooks County Sheriff's Department in Falfurrias, 120 kilometres inland from the Texas border, while I was waiting to speak to the deputy, the office assistant asked if I'd like to see the office's collection of photos of people who'd been found dead in the county in that year and the last. Some of the remains were skeletons. Sometimes they had just found teeth. Other bodies were bloated and unrecognisable or had their faces torn off by the coyotes, hogs and buzzards. Deputy Daniel Davila wandered in and said: "I see you're looking at our photo album." He said his office was losing its ability to deal with local crime because most of their work now involved illegals. Undocumented aliens had no trouble swimming, wading or clutching makeshift rafts to cross the Rio Grande. The Americans, overwhelmed by the breaches, still patrolled the border, but they had pulled back and were concentrating their efforts on the highways well inside US territory. Once on US soil, an illegal's real battle was to make it past the border checkpoint bottlenecks deeper inside Texas. Illegals were most often Mexicans, but ranchers were increasingly finding all sorts of nationalities wandering dazed in the scrub. Many of them paid their way by lugging backpacks of marijuana or cocaine for the Mexican cartels. Deputy Davila opened up a shipping container loaded with handmade wooden rucksacks for lugging dope, all loaded with weed.

"People say because we are not on the border, we really shouldn't be having problems," Davila said. "But over the years the volume has just been getting higher. We are getting a large number of immigrants in the bush, suffering dehydration or starvation. They're just trying to get across the border, into the United States, and then their journey begins." Davila took me on a tour of the local area, showing known spots near the highway where people hid while waiting to be collected. There were plastic water bottles and empty food tins. There was also discarded clothing, which they wore to protect themselves from the tearing scrub and the rattlesnakes. Wearing all this clothing, slogging through heavy sand in the heat, dramatically increased the chances of dehydration. This was America's equivalent of the seas off southern Java.

"It's kinda sad," said Davila. "I don't have any problem with these people coming here because they want to work, but they're shipped out like cattle. The coyote [the guide] will lead them through the bush. His job is to push that group as fast as they can go to a pick-up point. If there are any stragglers, or you start to have problems, or if you cramp up, it's not his problem. He doesn't care. He will push the ones who can move. He will leave the sick and the dehydrated." Those who could not pay the smuggler's fee – about US$1800 for a Mexican, higher for other nationalities

– had the option of loading up with backpacks of marijuana or cocaine.

"They're coming through the brush and you don't know what you're encountering," said the deputy. "You could be encountering a terrorist. They could be coming for a better life, they could be coming for something else. People say, 'Leave them alone, they're just after better lives.' At some point I don't disagree with that. But we have caught so many people from different places. People from El Salvador, Guatemala, China, Africa." He said he could not begin to guess how many people crossed through his county each year. "It's mind-boggling and a little scary."

At this time, June 2011, there were on average 5000 people thought to be crossing the US–Mexico border each week. Wherever there was human traffic, whatever the destination, there was high risk. In the previous year, ranchers in the Brooks County had found seventy-three bodies in the scrub. So far that year, the count was seventeen. Many more were lying out there unclaimed, and every rancher, Border Patrol officer, Texas Ranger and police officer knew that as they drove along the highways people were hiding in the bushes, waiting for them to pass so they could be collected by smugglers and make a dash for it.

"We had close to 500 deaths in this county alone since 2005," said Paul Vickers, a rancher and also the local vet in the town of Falfurrias, who once found his dog gnawing on a human skull in his yard. "Most of them are homicides, in my view. These people don't all just walk up here from the Rio Grande. They pay a fee to a travel agent in Mexico, who are gang members of the cartels. We have a big checkpoint just south of here, in the most active place in the nation for drug confiscation and illegal alien apprehension. They unload the people south of the checkpoint, and they all go over the fences, which are constantly being destroyed on a nightly basis.

"What'll happen [is that] a lot of the time the coyote will say, 'Walk that way for ten minutes and you'll be in Houston.'" Houston was 500 kilometres away. "They're lost," said Vickers. "They have no idea where they are. Three or four days later they're delirious, they've run out water and they lay down and die. I call it a homicide. Human smuggling is just as lucrative as the drug trade and this is the most active corridor for OTMs [Other Than Mexicans] on the whole southern border."

The Americans saw no gain in trying to control the debate; they only wanted to manage the traffic. There was an unspoken sense that if it were not for the drugs coming across, or the chance of the odd terrorist stumbling in, no one would bother trying to stem the flow. In the US, the cooks, the cleaners, the fast-food delivery people were all Latino. They were needed and wanted. In Mississippi, the governor's attempt to introduce tough anti-Latino laws had backfired. The crops weren't picked and the conservative farmers were irate. The illegals did the work no one else would do. In Australia, anyone who arrived by boat after 13 August 2012 and held a bridging visa while waiting for their claim to be processed was not permitted to work. This meant they required welfare support, which in turn caused them to be resented even more. In the US, illegals were seen as a potential resource; here, an economic imposition.

Some of the back rooms of the La Posada Hotel in Laredo look south to Mexico over the Rio Grande, which at this point is a concrete canal. The hotel is just a few hundred metres from a major border crossing. On the bridge, the cars and foot traffic were all coming one way – into the US. It was hard to know what country you were in. The customs officers all had Mexican surnames; and Laredo is a Spanish-speaking city. The only difference in the locations was that the rule of law was more or less intact on the US side, while across the Rio Grande the drug cartels were hanging people from bridges or cutting them up and leaving their heads in eskies.

In the hotel foyer, a Marine sergeant came walking by at a fast clip. I bailed him up with a rather loose question, which I felt half-stupid asking, but as it happened, he took to it. He spun a chair backwards, removed his fatigue cap and said: "What is this country? I'll tell you what it is. I do what I do in my yard, you do what you do in yours. And that's fine. Just don't do what you do in your yard in my yard. Because if you push me into a corner, I'm not going to be so law-abiding. Just across the border there, they got guns and drugs. As a matter of fact, so do we. We got bodies in the woods, too. We've got an old saying: 'I'd rather be judged by twelve than toted [carried in a casket] by six."

What does that mean? "It means I *will* use a gun to defend myself."

The sergeant was not so concerned about the infringement of his nation's sovereignty. It had gone beyond that. This man, a redneck from one perspective, was like many Americans sharply attuned to his individual rights. Here, where the US and Mexico were as one, he was more concerned with the encroachment of his own government than with foreigners. His right to bear arms and his right to free speech, which operated in tandem, were what he stood for, and stood to protect. They were the bedrock of his America. His country was an idea. It was very different to how the Australian frontal lobe thought of itself. We were untutored in the formative experience of revolution. We saw ourselves as a distinct physical manifestation in the form of a large, isolated island. We felt the need to protect the place, the thing. It was what defined us. We were less surefooted about our rights, though some certainly felt their freedoms had been challenged when John Howard banned all automatic weapons after the Port Arthur massacre, a decision the sergeant would have viewed as a shameful and colossal loss of personal liberty.

US politicians campaigned on keeping America great, or restoring it to greatness. But this had to be carefully managed to acknowledge that America was always changing. During the 2012 presidential campaign, the Republicans, after some early misjudged populist attacks on Latinos, backed right off. The Latino vote was becoming too strong. It was, however, too late for the Republicans, who in the election postmortem adjudged themselves as too white and middle-class, unrepresentative of modern America. They immediately vowed to recruit more Latino candidates for 2016. The most successful US administrations were the ones that did not seek to disturb underlying individual rights; and that now included not aggravating the great Latino working masses, for two reasons: those Latinos who were long-established residents, going back generations to even before the Declaration of Independence, were sick of being picked up by cops on the basis of their appearance and questioned about their legal status; and they were also sympathetic to newly arrived Latinos. The US was dealing with the issue by not making it an issue.

In Australia, we saw things more from an immediate policy perspective. We judged – and changed – governments on how they handled the big, live issues, taking a short-term view for fear of what the long-term picture might look like. We had not accepted that our nation was still a work-in-progress. A great number of Australians seemed to believe our country was now a finished product and the door ought to be bolted shut. We were not individual rights people and were not particularly interested in claims of mistreatment against unauthorised arrivals in our care. We trusted governments to do the right thing, yet were not alert to the steady intrusions on our own rights as citizens. We had never become acquainted with our own Constitution, a dull, unloved document that did not speak loudly for individuals and, due to the vagaries of common law, was susceptible to unpredictable interpretation. Our assumed freedom of speech, if it existed, was limited by growing controls on the ability to report and inform.

Under Labor, media conventions were introduced requiring anyone who visited an asylum detention centre to submit photos and their final story to the immigration department for approval. These were hardcore measures from the wrong side of the demilitarised zone, and most reporters, you would think, would not have accepted them. Immigration's media unit's head spokesman, Sandi Logan, in response to criticism, put out a list of media organisations that had complied with Immigration's terms in order to take a narrow look inside a detention centre. The list could be looked at two ways: a roll-call of shame; or an attempt by media to play along with Immigration in the hope of snagging some decent information, which was rarely forthcoming. The most that could be expected was a note attached to a thrown rock.

Submitting material intended for publication to the government was necessary, it was explained, to protect the privacy of asylum seekers. It was fair enough, on one hand, that if someone had their image or name published, it might put them at risk should they be sent home. On the other, the fact that they would be at risk at home seemed to support their application for protection. But in the case of the Sri Lankans, especially, who were being sent home without having their photos or names published in the media, the Australian government's view that they were not at risk from a ruthless Colombo was callous fiction.

There was another unspoken reason, based on a fear that individual stories – particularly those involving asylum children – could give rise to an unwanted national compassion. But the grim truth was that as much as you might complain about restrictive policy, there was little interest in asylum tales. The public had tired of them. The media covered the issue on the basis of how much mess the government could make of each new solution. The sympathy that the government feared might be unleashed did not exist.

LITTLE AUSSIE MIGRANT

Rudd, after his second coming, began to understand the deep popular resentment towards asylum seekers. Back in late 2007 when he had ordered the offshore facilities to be closed, he probably thought he could take the people with him, believing them tired after the long years of John Howard and wanting a more compassionate Australia. His apology to the stolen generations was reported as an across-the-board triumph, though very easy to give; and no matter how heartfelt, everyone needed it done and dusted; we really needed to move onto something else. Perhaps Rudd thought ending the Pacific Solution fell into the same category. If so, he was wrong. Instead of finishing something, he started something. It took time for boat numbers to build, which coincided with a drop in Rudd's popularity as the polls showed sharp dissatisfaction in response to his handling of the *Oceanic Viking* stand-off of October 2009. That event had begun well for Rudd – when President Yudhoyono agreed to his request to take into detention seventy-eight Sri Lankan asylum seekers whom an Australian Customs vessel had pulled from waters inside Indonesia's search and rescue zone – but fell apart when they refused to disembark in Indonesia. In April 2010, Rudd temporarily suspended the processing of Sri Lankan and Afghan asylum claims, for six and three months respectively, in what he claimed was a response to improving conditions in both countries. It was an attempt to get him through the coming election period. Government policy became a series of rolling missives from the Department of the Prime Minister and Cabinet to bug-eyed immigration heads to come up with quick deterrent solutions. Then Gillard rolled Rudd and she got the worst of the boats.

When John Howard had his wave of arrivals, he railed against asylum seekers on the public stage, built offshore centres, excised the northern shores and islands from the mainland, introduced temporary protection visas, and dragged out processing times. Howard's policies so disgusted his backbench that he was forced to head off a revolt, led by Victorian MP Petro Georgiou, who won concessions that saw women, children and families released from mandatory detention into community housing, and the processing time for visas halved from six to three months.

A person in mandatory detention, onshore or off, was never as visible as an arriving boat. Gillard understood much better than Rudd the depth of Australian public disquiet on the boats. It was Gillard who in 2003, as shadow minister for immigration, had headlined a media release attacking the Howard government: "Another boat on the way, another policy failure." If Rudd was an internationalist, Gillard exhibited a slightly overwrought patriotism, common enough among first-generation migrant peoples.

Gillard did not mention asylum seekers in her first address after rolling Rudd on 24 June 2010, when she talked about the key issues of her coming leadership. She was not comfortable with it, and it was not because she was afraid of showing sympathy. Rather it appeared she was reluctant to reveal how little she had, which might damage her standing with a frustrated corner of voters (once upon a time called the "doctors' wives") who thought Labor was too hard on asylum seekers. Gillard took a different approach by creating her own slow-boat family narrative, repeatedly referring to the tale of her parents who came from a small Welsh town, arrived knowing no one and toiled hard to make it in Australia. The point was that her parents had done it the right way.

On 24 June 2010, the day she became prime minister: "I grew up in a home of hard-working parents..."

On 6 July 2010, in her Moving Australia Forward speech to the Lowy Institute: "That hard-working Australians who themselves are doing it tough want to know that refugees allowed to settle here are not singled out for special treatment. That people like my own parents, who have worked hard all their lives, the thing that they can't abide is the idea that others might get an inside track to special privileges."

On 10 July 2010, in an address in Adelaide: "I'm standing before you today because of the brave decision [her parents] made in 1966 to migrate to Australia ... [W]ithout higher education, obtaining even their moderate level of prosperity involved a lot of hard work. For my mother it meant cooking and scrubbing pots in a Salvation Army aged care home. And for my father it meant demanding work and frequent nightshifts, as a nurse in a psychiatric hospital. Their experience has instilled in me clear beliefs about the importance and the value of work that I hold to this day."

No one minded that her parents were ten-pound Poms. No one cared. The constantly repeated yarn that her parents had worked so hard, and were supposedly representatives of Australian exceptionalism, thrilled no one. It was an old story. It was fifty years old. Everyone knew a ten-pound Pom. The king of Aussie bloke music, Jimmy Barnes, was one. He didn't go on about it. Acknowledging history was one thing, thrashing it another. So why did Gillard so often refer to it? It was not news to any Australian that parents in the '60s, wherever they came from, worked hard. But it did allow her to set the scene for her first injudicious move against asylum seekers. In the Lowy Institute speech, Gillard announced her East Timor Solution, having first provided the backdrop of her parents' orderly migration: "In recent days I have discussed with President Ramos Horta of East Timor the possibility of establishing a regional processing centre for the purpose of receiving and processing irregular entrants to the region. The purpose would be to ensure that people smugglers have no product to sell. A boat ride to Australia would just be a ticket back to the regional processing centre. It would be to ensure that everyone is subject to a consistent, fair assessment process. It would be to ensure that arriving by boat does not give anybody an advantage in the likelihood that they would end up settling in Australia or other countries of the region. It would, of course, have to be properly run, properly auspiced, properly structured."

The next day, Gillard was in Darwin, inspecting naval boats at the Larrakeyah base with David Bradbury, then Labor's federal Member for Lindsay, standing behind her in every shot. Bradbury, whose seat took in part of landlocked western Sydney, had been complaining loudest that he'd be thrown out if the boats weren't stopped. He seemed to have picked up on the true mood of the electorate and now had Gillard's ear, finely attuned to the dangers lurking in western Sydney, where voters feared their suburbs were a final destination for Muslim refugees.

Gillard, inexperienced or badly advised, had contacted President José Ramos Horta rather than her notoriously touchy counterpart, Prime Minister Xanana Gusmão. The garrulous, welcoming Ramos Horta held a largely ceremonial post; and he still felt in Australia's close personal debt, having been airlifted to Darwin and given life-saving medical treatment after rebels shot him in the back in 2008 (which they did largely because of promises he had made to them, which he was unable to keep). We in the press took the Airnorth flight to Dili and found a put-upon Gusmão and a furious East Timorese cabinet. Ramos Horta had made himself scarce. Gusmão had never shown Australia much warmth, in part due to his view that Australia had hogged oil and gas in the Timor Sea; and his current anger was engaged by Woodside's decision not to pipe oil and gas from the Timor Sea direct to East Timor, which would have created jobs for his people. Gusmão, master of the slowly revealed insult, declared he had no position on the Gillard proposal but would leave it to Ramos Horta to negotiate with Australia while he went off to gauge the mood of the Timorese people. Gusmão gave Ramos Horta neither diplomatic nor moral support as he sent him off for discussions with Australian officials from the Department of Foreign Affairs and Trade (DFAT), who'd been desperately scrambled to Dili and who now knew they were dealing with the wrong man. The East Timorese parliament condemned the move and Ramos Horta and Gillard were left to hang in the breeze.

Gillard, in her search for a solution, and for political survival, now fingered the map and came up with Malaysia, a more or less unfriendly semi-ally with a very poor record on human rights, which thrashed prisoners with canes, had a police force with a stop-and-search policy that mirrored South Africa's Apartheid-era passbook requirements, did not recognise Israel, kept unfavoured citizens in a state of fear and unease, punished homosexuality, did not run free and fair elections, controlled the media absolutely, controlled the judiciary, dealt with the outspoken using subversion charges, and appeared to be a preferred address for questionable individuals on the regional terror map. Gillard and Chris Bowen decided Malaysia was a good idea. Australia still maintained a presence at an airbase called Butterworth, a legacy of times when Malaysia was thought a more worthwhile friend than Indonesia, during the period of *konfrontasi.* And now Malaysia, not a party to the 1951 Refugee Convention and without systems to regulate the status and rights of refugees, was going to help us with our asylum-seeker problem.

Yet Malaysia, more than any other regional country, had helped create the problem with its shockingly lax visa controls. Sixty per cent of boat arrivals came through Malaysia, yet it was Indonesia's sovereign interests that were most affected by Malaysia's lack of control over both plane arrivals and secretive boat departures. From Kuala Lumpur it was a short ride across the Strait of Malacca to Sumatra, or from Johor Bahru in southern Malaysia, an easy night ride in an overloaded speedboat to small nearby Indonesian islands, or to one of the so-called bunker ships which idled in international waters and gathered asylum seekers in their hulls for delivery to Indonesia.

The proposed deal was that Australia would accept 4000 UNHCR-registered refugees from Malaysia, over four years, in return for 800 irregular maritime arrivals who had arrived on Christmas Island. Gillard and Bowen called the signing of the transfer deal, in July

2011, a "groundbreaking arrangement," which demonstrated "the resolve of Australia and Malaysia to break the people smugglers' business model, stop them profiting from human misery, and stop people risking their lives at sea." If Malaysia, home to 90,000 (mostly Burmese) registered refugees, another 10,000 asylum seekers, and more than a million outsider citizens of undetermined status, really did have any such resolve, it had dealt with the problem with mass round-ups, whippings and deportations.

It was curious that Malaysia had never asked Australia, as a regional friend, for assistance to deal with its own massive refugee problem. A cynical view was that Malaysia had used refugees to create a massive underpaid manufacturing and servant underclass, which elevated the Malaysian masters right where they wanted to be. Now, for the $300 million offered by Australia, Malaysia would get a tiny reduction in its refugee numbers. Australia would raise its annual humanitarian intake by 1000 per year, while deporting a handful from Christmas Island. Bowen's claim that this would break the smugglers made no sense. We would send to Malaysia the equivalent of just 200 people, per year, over four years, when many thousands were arriving annually. It was easy to see how Malaysia could hardly say no; harder to stomach Labor's low reckoning of the electorate's intelligence.

Bowen said he consulted the UNHCR on Malaysia, which meant that he, as a courtesy, advised them of the plan. There were some laughably terrible fine-print details attached to the deal. One was that involuntary transferees to Malaysia would receive counselling en route to Kuala Lumpur in the charter plane; and if they then refused to disembark upon arrival in KL, they would be escorted to the door of the plane and handed directly to Malaysian authorities. Another clause appeared to have been inserted by the Malaysians, who having already got a good deal, decided to ram it home. It was that if a transferee was removed to Malaysia, but then took another boat to Australia, their second transfer (and any subsequent transfer after that) to Malaysia was not to be counted as part of the 800. In other words, Australia couldn't pass the same bloke off twice. It was hard to believe the Australian Labor Party had come up with this rubbish.

Abbott's position was that the Malaysia Solution was "a dud deal for Australia and a cruel deal for boat people"; Scott Morrison, at that time a supporter of open government, a free media and human rights, condemned the proposal at a press conference as Abbott stood by his side: "Imagine taking boat people from Australia to Malaysia where they will be exposed almost inevitably to the prospect of caning," he said. "They will be detained, they will be tagged, they will be let out into the community – and in the Malaysian community, people of uncertain immigration status are treated very, very harshly indeed and what is supposed to protect people in Malaysia from caning and other very harsh treatment is this tag. What this government is proposing is to take boat people from Christmas Island, detain them, tag them and then expect that they're not going to get caned."

A month later, after an expedited High Court action initiated by David Manne from the Refugee and Immigration Legal Centre, the nation's most effective and dispassionate cross-examiner and dismantler of bad asylum law, the court issued this statement: "Today the High Court held invalid the Minister for Immigration and Citizenship's [Bowen's] declaration of Malaysia as a country to which asylum seekers who entered Australia at Christmas Island can be taken for processing of their asylum claims." The court found that Malaysia, which was not a signatory to the Refugee Convention and had no formal protocols on refugees, did not meet the standards required by Australia's *Migration Act.* The Malaysia Solution was dead.

In December 2011, Gillard wrote to Abbott urging him to support changes to legislation that would permit offshore processing, including in Malaysia. She warned that Australia had no effective deterrents in place and that the number of boats was likely to rise. She was prepared to reconvene parliament, if the Opposition would change its mind and support Labor policy. "The fact of the matter is that both parties agree on the need for offshore processing," Gillard wrote. "It is in the national interest to resolve this matter, even if we do not agree on the preferred policy response." Gillard urged Abbott to put his man Morrison with her man Bowen to talk things through and find a way to break the impasse.

Abbott's letter in response, bristling with hostility and sarcasm, stands on record as among his least edifying moments. Abbott was unwilling to assist Gillard's minority government on the boats unless strictly on his own terms. Noting the recent surge, condemning the government's announcement that boat arrivals would be released into the community on bridging visas, with work rights, Abbott's position was clear: the dangerous monsoon seas were coming and people were being attracted to Christmas Island with the hope of turning those bridging visas into permanent residencies. "Since you and Mr Rudd dismantled the policies that worked, there have been almost two boats a week on average," Abbott wrote. "The number of people arriving by boat has more recently doubled, to more than 310 people per week. This is more people arriving in a week than in the last six years of the Howard Government."

Gillard would not back down on Malaysia and Abbott would not back down, full stop. It had been difficult to gauge whether the Coalition was truly incensed about Malaysia's human-rights record, or just thought it was a bad deal for Australia. Now it was clear. Referring to the rolling crises in the overcrowded detention centres, demanding a full return to Howard-era policy, Abbott delivered a foul line that confirmed any hope Australians might have had for joint leadership on the issue was vain. "This is a problem you have created and that it is your responsibility to solve," Abbott told Gillard.

Such was the state of the Australian parliament. All the talk about deaths at sea and concerns about Malaysia stood second to Abbott's political interest. Gillard refused to consider an option that did not include Malaysia. Labor had made the big mistakes on asylum policy, yet it was Abbott's refusal to even talk through a possible solution with Gillard's government that sent a loud message to smugglers and asylum seekers: we're in bedlam, come on down. The situation dragged for almost another year under Gillard, as boat numbers really started to climb.

***

In late June 2012, ten boats came in one week. Two of those sank off Christmas Island. Some 20,000 asylum seekers had arrived since Rudd had dismantled Howard's Pacific Solution and the problem was about to get a lot worse: more than 25,000 people would arrive by boat, under Gillard, between June 2012 and June 2013. There was an argument that we'd lost perspective. Other countries – Italy, France, Greece and the US – had greater asylum arrival pressures. But we were not those places.

Other countries, such as the UK and the US, suffered much higher death tolls than Australia in Afghanistan, but we still treated every digger's death as a matter of front-page national significance. We grieved and we questioned the value of that person's death. In the UK and the US, a soldier's death no longer rated more than a few centimetres in a newspaper. We believed ourselves to be both country and community, and we were trying to hold on to that belief, perhaps naively and hopelessly so. It was not about being a white enclave; nor was it purely anti-Muslim. There was a broad understanding that Islam itself was corrosively and viciously divided, but for reasons that defied our easy comprehension. It was forgivable that we did not wish to gain a firsthand understanding. We were entitled to know who was coming, and we were entitled to detain them for a reasonable time in order to process them. Politicians were entitled to factor public opinion into their decisions, but they also needed to control and support the numerous frontline agencies, which were now overrun. Under such circumstances, the professional, compassionate care expected of Australia as a sophisticated and wealthy First World country was being compromised. Politicians were also required to lead. Labor never liked having an open conversation with the public. Abbott's people would take the view that it was too late for conversation.

Another statistic that pro-asylum voices claimed pointed to Australia's lack of perspective on the boats was that most asylum seekers came by plane. It was true, or it had been until the 2012–13 surge, but

Professor Mary Crock from the University of Sydney – who seemed to see both sides of the debate – told *Dateline* during the *Oceanic Viking* stand-off: "People who come by plane are at least processed to some extent – they present their passports to get into the country, and so on. Whereas people who come by boat come without any documentation of any kind and they haven't had any health or character checking at all. So there are obvious concerns that are very valid for governments."

ASIO did not have a Christmas Island Situation Room where agents waved their palms over holographic computers and touch-screened to life the individual stories of 25,000 mostly undocumented people who'd arrived in the past twelve months. Trying to gather background information on that number of people was a considerable undertaking given the starting point was an uncorroborated statement from a stranger. If it was "Orwellian" for ASIO to check someone out, too bad. We had a problem. It seemed to count for little that Australia was in the top three countries taking the world's annually resettled refugees and asylum seekers. We could take more, and Gillard did raise the intake. But what was most needed was genuine regional cooperation. For that to have any chance, political cooperation was first needed at home. Abbott was determined for his political benefit that the matter not be resolved.

With Gillard unable to muster support from the Greens to pass any change to the *Migration Act,* independent

NSW MP Rob Oakeshott, a believer in his own special healing powers, proposed a compromise private member's bill that sought to change the *Migration Act* to permit the immigration minister to transfer any boat arrival to an "offshore assessment country," being any of the huge sweep of fifty-plus nations (which included dysfunctional nations such as Afghanistan, Syria, Iran and Iraq) that were signatories to the Bali Process. This was the forum conceived under Howard in 2002 to combat people-smuggling across the region – and world – with improved intelligence sharing. Over ten years of annual conferences there had been little to show, particularly in relation to the most important member nation, Indonesia. While the Oakeshott bill would have seen Nauru and Manus Island reopened, it would also have allowed Labor to pursue the Malaysia Solution again. Oakeshott's bill had the impassioned support of Gillard and Bowen, but if Oakeshott imagined he had just enough political distance from Labor for the Coalition to go for it, he was wrong. Abbott was not going to forget that Oakeshott had helped deliver Gillard her minority government in 2010.

The Coalition refused to contemplate Malaysia. Bronwyn Bishop called it a "trade in human flesh"; Joe Hockey said the deal would see unaccompanied children sent to Malaysia and that would happen "over my dead body." The bill failed in the Senate.

Gillard, with nowhere else to turn, called an inquiry, commissioning former defence chief Angus Houston to come up with some answers. The report was compiled over just six weeks, and it showed. The general reaction was: "Short on detail." Abbott pre-empted the report's delivery, saying he didn't particularly care what it said, because he already had a border-protection plan. Abbott spoke too soon: none of the key points contradicted Coalition policy. It recommended the reopening of Nauru and Manus Island; did not rule out turning back the boats when the time was right; did not consider the Malaysia Solution as currently workable; advocated application of a "no advantage" principle, meaning a person who came by boat would not get a visa ahead of someone waiting in a refugee camp; and recommended that Australia's humanitarian intake be immediately increased from 13,750 to 20,000 places (a position Abbott had said he would consider during debate on the Oakeshott bill). The Gillard government accepted the panel's recommendations. The problem was they did nothing to stop the boats. It would take the most part of another year, and one sentence from Kevin Rudd, to slow them to a crawl.

THE SMUGGLING COAST

After parting ways with Ali Reza and the city of Cisarua, I headed down to the southern coast of Java with photographer Ardiles Rante. The idea was to gauge the impact of Rudd's announcement. Some people in Cisarua had said they would still be going by boat, others that they would now abandon the quest. It was loose polling. The true effect could be measured only by finding out if boats were still leaving. This had to be tempered with the fact that groups of passengers had already been quarantined, in readiness for travel. There was no chance that smugglers would inform their passengers of Rudd's announcement. If they knew, they might demand their money back. The smugglers didn't want that kind of confrontation.

On the way down to the coast, Ardiles rang ahead to a newspaper contact in Sukabumi, a small city inland from the southern coast, thought to be a major junction for asylum seekers moving down to the coast. His contact told him that some hundred or so people had been apprehended south of Sukabumi the day before. The information was vague. No one from the newspaper had gone to take photos. Asylum seekers were of no interest to the Indonesian media. It was an Australian story. We drove on to Pelabuhan Ratu, about 400 kilometres directly north of Christmas Island, a place well known to Australian surfers. It was not the closest point between Java and Christmas

Island, but close enough. We talked with some tuna fishermen, who went farthest out to sea. They said the asylum boats didn't leave from Pelabuhan Ratu; the port was too public. It was suggested we might look further east, to a small village called Cidaun.

In Pelabuhan Ratu, we met the deputy police commander, Major Philemon Ginting, who had detained the asylum seekers as they came into town the day before. There were eighty, not a hundred, he said. He said they were all from Afghanistan, but I would learn that this was the term used for any stranger from South Asia or the Middle East. Major Ginting said police had received a tip-off about two open trucks seen passing the military base, in the hills over Pelabuhan Ratu. The two drivers had been questioned, saying they'd each been paid US$150 to transport the asylum seekers to a remote beach. They'd claimed not to know who their employers were. Major Ginting said there was no reason to hold the drivers, because it was not a criminal offence in Indonesia to drive a truck. Holding the passengers was just as hard. The police had no desire to catch asylum seekers because it was a time-wasting game of catch and release, but it seemed there was a directive from higher up, in Jakarta, to make some arrests. These cops were the antithesis of the Malaysian stop-and-search head-crackers: they didn't want to hurt or frighten anyone, but nor did they want to feed them. Because that's what always happened. They'd detain a group, but the police had no budget for asylum seekers, so the cops had to reach into their own pockets out of human decency. They didn't like it – they hated it – but felt they had to. Then they'd put in a call to Immigration to come and get them, but their budget was also minus zero. Once Immigration took them off police hands, they were sent straight back to Cisarua on a bus. There, they would regroup, cool their heels, while their smugglers devised a different plan to get them to a boat. To make matters worse, Ginting described the asylum seekers as being angry with police for being detained, suggesting they had been assured by their smugglers that they had police protection.

Major Ginting insisted his district was not a major departure point. So where? He suggested we look east, to Cidaun. "They usually offer us money to let them go ahead," Major Ginting said. "They offer $1000. We have never taken it. But the police here earn $400 a month. What do you think?" He studied me. "Is that a lot of money? Would some police take it?"

Ginting said Australia and Indonesia had the same problem. "Your country can't send them back. Same for Indonesia. I have spoken to them. I believe they are victims of war, but I also think it's their dream to go to Australia. So I don't think they're just victims. Their friends in Australia tell them how beautiful it is." Like the Australian Federal Police in Jakarta, he disputed the notion of meticulously organised syndicates. "Never," he said. "That does not happen.

It is small groups trying to find smugglers." So why, given the problems for under-resourced police, did they even bother making the arrest? A more senior officer leaned in and said: "We have orders from the president to stop them."

If this information was correct, Yudhoyono or someone senior had sent an instruction, presumably to help Rudd during his election fight. Yudhoyono had tried to help Rudd before, during *Oceanic Viking;* and he had, at least according to Rudd's office, if not the Indonesians, responded to a request to end visas-on-arrivals for Iranians. But why had Australia not gone directly to Indonesia for assistance in setting up an offshore processing centre, rather than playing in the periphery with Nauru, PNG, East Timor and Malaysia? Perhaps Australia had done this, but the rejection was too humiliating to report. Any hope for a genuine regional solution rested with Indonesia, the final stepping stone to Australia. It is true Indonesia is not a signatory to the 1951 Refugee Convention, and it was easy to understand why John Howard, during the time of *Tampa* in 2001, had never made such an approach: Australia had, two years earlier, raised an international force to liberate East Timor from Indonesia. (And indeed, perhaps hoping for a show of gratitude, Howard had asked East Timor to take the people from the *Tampa,* a request which was rejected.) But we'd come together with Indonesia since then, sharing resources and pain after the 2002 Bali bombings, us sharing theirs in the 2004 Boxing Day tsunami. There had been the Bali Process forums, where the entire region apparently agreed that asylum seekers were a shared problem. Why did neither Howard, in his better times with Indonesia, or Labor, from 2007, seek a one-on-one solution with Indonesia? "The Indonesian Solution." Those words would have been the most convincing political statement any Australian government could ever deliver to Australian voters on asylum seekers.

Indonesia had never sought to run a naval blockade of the asylum-seeker boats departing so regularly from the south coast of Java. It stood to reason that most boats were leaving from this vicinity. The Bali Process was invisible down here, and Australia's expectations were in complete contrast to Indonesia's. We prayed they would stop them; they said good riddance.

We left Pelabuhan Ratu behind, concluding – partly based on the presence of Australians surfing beach breaks that crashed close to shore onto round, black rocks – that this was not a suitable place to launch an asylum boat, unless they were leaving from the still waters of the fishing port itself, which seemed too public and brazen. Heading east and then south, and closer to Christmas Island, we came to Ujung Genteng, a resort town that spread itself thinly over long kilometres of beach frontage. It was a place of small sand-blasted hotels and shacks, spaced well apart from each other on the wasted shores, a few of which hung red lanterns in their eaves to indicate service to evening customers. But in July, there were very few people around. It was a desolate place.

We encountered a naval officer, Dendi Heryandi, outside his local base, a two-room outpost that served as headquarters to the local six-man navy unit. We learned that this building, which served as both office and living quarters on one of the busiest points on the smuggling coast, had not been built with Indonesian defence money but with donations begged from local businesses. They shared one inflatable boat, although the forty-horsepower outboard was in for repairs. Asked whether they had a radar, Dendi laughed. Here, at the closest point to Christmas Island, they did not even have two-way radios. Naval communications were limited to their personal mobile phones. Dendi said that last night three suspicious vehicles had arrived at the small river mouth nearby, where the local fishing boats put to sea. They had sped away when someone approached the vehicles. Dendi pointed to a nearby hotel, where a man they believed to be Middle Eastern, and dressed in the manner of a cleric, had taken extended residence in one of the rooms and was under casual observation by the naval team. There were no grounds, so far, Dendi said, to question him.

Dendi took us down a track to meet the head of the small naval unit, Commander Ridwan, who was doing a night shift guarding the local turtle sanctuary from poachers. On the way, we passed a Hazara man on a motorbike. It certainly felt as if we had arrived on the smuggling coast. Ridwan, ordering coffee and passing clove cigarettes, said that there was a boat anchored off a remote beach about forty kilometres back up the coast towards Pelabuhan Ratu. It was being watched by local villagers, who were his eyes and ears around the area. He said the boat had come from the west, in neighbouring Banten Province. He suspected it was ready to collect a load of asylum seekers. Commander Ridwan was keeping one eye on the boat, but protecting turtles was his main concern. Indonesia had become very worried about what Indonesia was doing to itself with its monoculture palm-oil plantations and overfishing. This was not vague background hum; environmentalism informed the conversations of so many Indonesians, looking to save what was left.

We asked Ridwan if he could spare an officer to take us to where the boat was anchored, and he agreed. As we began organising motorbikes for the morning, to get through rough tracks to the remote beach, Ridwan rang his village contact for an update. The boat had gone. It had collected no passengers but was headed south. He suspected it would likely skirt Ujung Genteng, out of view of the coastline, and head east along the coast. The most likely passenger pick-up point was the village of Cidaun, about 160 kilometres away.

***

We were accompanied on our drive by a junior intelligence officer, A. The three-hour drive became six due to road repairs and the trail of trucks loaded with so-called iron sand, which was being mined directly from the beaches. It was the cause of much local angst. Like the turtles, the damaged beaches far outweighed any concerns about boats leaving from this coast.

We arrived in the village of Cidaun in the early evening and met in the home of a local man who worked for Fisheries. We learned from him that a boat had set off for Australia that morning. He claimed not to know much about the movement of asylum seekers. He summoned a local fisherman, a small and older man named Obin, who with huge hands took a tin of chocolate-flavoured condensed milk and made careful Spirograph patterns on white bread, while making it clear he resented being asked questions. He did not particularly wish to talk to or look at an Australian journalist, directing reluctant answers to the man from Fisheries. Obin agreed that many asylum boats left from Cidaun; but, surely, everyone knew this? He said the fishermen would ferry the passengers to the bigger boats in their double-outrigger praus. He confirmed that a boat had left that morning. The asylum seekers had arrived the night before in a series of vans, stopping on the roadside just east of the town, where they were marched several kilometres through a small nature reserve down to a quiet beach. Locals profited in various ways, either by using their boats, watching the roads or acting as guides and porters on the march down to the beach. Asked why the local police station in the village seemed unaware of this activity, Obin shrugged. Asked when the next boat was to leave, Obin said he did not know. But it was unlikely one would leave for days or weeks. Obin said that whenever a departure was imminent, the whole village tensed up in anticipation of the passengers. He said there was no tension in the village, not tonight, because there were no passengers coming.

That night we slept in a clapped-out motel. Waking late, we wandered down to the beach, where the fishing boats were moored off a small beach by an intricate system of long ropes to keep them from crashing into each other in the waves. Towards Australia, the skies looked heavy. And so did the locals, who did not seem pleased to see us. Ardiles returned with news: a boat had left that morning, in daylight. Obin, nowhere to be seen, had been less than forthcoming. We could see a dot on the far horizon. The boat was on its way. I filed a news story stating that the first confirmed boat had left Indonesia since Rudd's 19 July announcement. And we watched the sea. By midday, a fierce wind was howling from the south up on to the Java shores, meaning the boat must have been lurching directly into it. From what we could learn, it was an inter-island ferry, not made for such seas. The intel officer, A., learned it was the same boat that had been under observation near Ujung Genteng.

We loitered for a time in Cidaun and decided to give up. Now that our presence was known, there was little chance the smugglers would use Cidaun for some days to come. It was obvious we were in one of Indonesia's busiest set-off points for Australia. It had probably been that way for five years, since Rudd relaxed policy. Yet whenever you spoke to Australian authorities about likely departure points in Indonesia, they were vague, declining to reveal locations, even after a boat ran into trouble and sank off Christmas Island. It was as though it was too much information to share, too valuable an operational secret. As I guessed it, Australia knew the exact departure points, but it would embarrass Indonesia to name specific locations, because it would reveal how little Indonesia did to intervene; and embarrass Australia too, because it would show how little influence we really had in Indonesia.

A BOAT GOES DOWN

We departed Cidaun and drove inland, north to Sukabumi, where we were to drop A., the intel officer. A. said the lack of funding for police and military meant the boats would never be stopped at the Indonesian end. He could see Australia's problem, but he was more worried about the Indonesian fishermen who died at sea doing the work of the smugglers, and for coastal citizens who were terrified of the effect the smugglers had on their communities. The smugglers were an unknown quantity in terms of their propensity for violence, and they were presumably receiving assistance from local authorities.

A. told us of Nyai Roro Kadul, the Queen of the Southern Sea in local Sundanese lore, depicted in local paintings and wall murals as a beautiful woman. She had the power to raise great tempests, but these were not an indication of her fury. "No, she never gets angry," said A. "She protects and gives prosperity. She is the queen of our safety. If there is a fisherman missing, or an accident, then maybe they have been called to meet the queen. If there is a big problem, if there is a curse on my family, I will ask her for help. She assists with good directions in life, and helps me to be a good Muslim." In the most transcendent moments, Nyai Roro Kadul would take the form of a man's wife during sex.

After we dropped A., a call came through from another intel officer we had met along the way: a boat had gone down off Cidaun. We drove back, arriving on the outskirts of the village at 2 or 3a.m. People were up and about. We noticed life jackets hanging off the front of several porches. Driving on a little further, we came to a small town hall, all lit up. People in uniform were gathered out the front. We walked in and saw numerous Sri Lankans collapsed on the floor, most of them sleeping in sarongs the locals had given them. The one or two Sri Lankans who were awake did not speak English. The only non-Sri Lankan was Soheil, aged twenty-three, who was beside himself. "Sixty-one Iranians are dead," he said. "I am the only one back." It was the morning of 24 July.

Soheil said he was from Abadan City, in Iran, meaning he was an Arab Iranian. He said they had come to Indonesia less than a month before taking the boat. The previous morning, passengers had been taken to a jungle trail, just east of Cidaun, and ferried on small boats out to a bigger boat, but after several hours of steaming towards Australia the boat got into trouble. "The sea very hard, the sea no good," he said. "The ship break. The captain he go to small boat, no help me, no help children, no help baby. He go." The captain had abandoned ship and saved himself. Soheil estimated there were 170 on the boat, mostly from Iran and Sri Lanka. I counted thirty-four survivors in the hall. This appeared to be all that was left of the boat we'd seen on the horizon yesterday morning.

Unknown to Soheil, there were many more survivors. We were directed to drive further to the village of Cidaun itself, where there was a similar scene inside another town hall, with people lying everywhere, in deep shock. There were two bodies lying on tables, covered with sarongs: one belonged to a girl, said to be aged twelve; and another to an older woman. Ali, twenty-four, was crouched against a wall, exhausted. The dead woman was his mother, Samirah, aged forty-six. With Ali was his sister, Maha, aged six, brothers Abdullah and Mohammad, aged sixteen and twenty-three, and his uncle, Yusef. I looked at Maha, the youngest in the family, who was staring at nothing in a state of uncomprehending trauma.

Yusef was on the phone, weeping as he broke the news to home about Samirah's death. Ali, whose family had also originally come from Abadan City, gave me his account of what had happened: "We were six hours underway, but the boat that was given to us was no good. According to us, this was on purpose. There was a hole in the boat, but they did not call the coastguard. We called our smuggler to send boats to save [us] and he kept saying he would. The boat kept sinking." At some point the captain, a Sri Lankan, gave up and turned around, heading back for Java. At best estimates, they came within five kilometres of the shore. "We got some waves," Ali said, "and in a few seconds it broke from the middle and sank. We were in the sea for six hours with a rope and a tube, no life jackets. There were some life jackets, but all the Iranians had none. People died instantly, kids died instantly."

Ali's family had planned to migrate to Australia en masse, but only some had been able to secure visas. Those without visas were on the boat. In Jakarta, two weeks earlier, they had met Iranian smugglers whom Ali named as Naseem, the broker, and Abu Yunis, who ran the operation. He said as they prepared to travel, the mobile phones that had been taken from them were given back.

Yusef, Ali's uncle, was breaking into the conversation, despairing as he gestured towards Samirah's body on the table. Ali told how his mum died in the sea; how they kept her corpse afloat and brought it to shore: "Mum had a heart attack and died. She survived for four hours and then had a heart attack and died." The smugglers had told them it would be easy. "They make it sound perfect," Ali said. "But once you give them the money, things change. Their phones switch off." Ali echoed what Soheil had said, and I would hear something similar from many who were on that boat: as they sank, there was a small fishing boat and a larger police vessel floating nearby, watching, declining to help.

The district commander of the Cianjur police, Dedy Kusama Bakti, was organising the rescue and trying to get a handle on how many were on the boat. Some said 150, others 175. Smugglers kept no manifests, so it was impossible for Commander Dedy to know when all the passengers, dead or alive, had been accounted for. It would turn out around 210 were jammed onto the vessel, but the precise number would never be known.

As local fishermen began to search the seas in their small boats – some of them no doubt the same men who had transported these people to the doomed asylum boat – a small clinic down the road had become both a makeshift emergency department and a morgue. An Iranian woman with dyed blonde hair was half-carried into the clinic. She was unable to walk without assistance and was shaking uncontrollably. I asked the overwhelmed local doctor, the only doctor, who gave her name as Vivi, what was wrong with the shaking woman, whose name I noted as Fatemah. Dr Vivi said she was in a state of diabetic shock. Vivi said there was no insulin in Cidaun.

More people were being pulled from the sea and arriving, dead and alive, in ambulances at the clinic. They were putting body bags in a separate building across the way. Every time a new one arrived, people would rush over, unzip the bag and new screams would come. One man who had just found someone – his brother or his friend, I did not know – collapsed into my arms and wept. I held the huge man as he rocked, saying, "Thank you, thank you, thank you." At that point I started getting passably upset and noticed that Ardiles, who wore long hair, was using his head scarf to wipe away tears in between dutifully shooting the despairing scene which we, as journalists, had the mixed fortune to have all to ourselves, all day.

Survivors were begging to use my phone, calling numbers in Iran or England, then hanging up and waiting for someone to call back on my number. Certain people all around the world knew about this boat, and were counting on its safe arrival on Christmas Island. When the phone rang, someone would recognise the incoming number and wail the bad news.

In a small back room of the clinic, a dead baby had lain all morning wrapped in a white shroud. It was decided it was time to shift the baby inland to a proper hospital morgue. Vinothini, a very young mother, stumbled in grief, supported by her husband, Vimalarasu, as paramedics carried the yellow body bag holding their one-year-old son, Kishanlh, to an ambulance. A young girl was brought from the sea to the clinic. She looked to be aged three or four. Her eyes were rolling to the back of her head and she was shuddering wildly. All you could see were the whites of her eyes. Dr Vivi inserted a drip as her parents slapped her wrists and massaged her feet, working tirelessly to rouse her. It looked hopeless to me. The little girl appeared to be brain-damaged from being underwater too long.

I stood in the doorway of the clinic, talking to two Sri Lankan women. One was Dhanusa, aged thirty-four, from Sri Lanka. She said her three children, aged twelve, ten and seven, and her husband were all gone, taken by the sea. She said that after the boat, wickedly overloaded by the smugglers, nosedived and broke at the seams, a vessel had pulled alongside as she struggled in the sea. "One ship near us," she said in broken English. "Not save, not care." The story kept coming up of another boat watching the asylum vessel sink, but not helping. Other witnesses would say the captain of the asylum vessel, a Sri Lankan man, had arranged through the smuggler network for a small fishing boat to be sent to rescue himself, abandoning the others. He was seen swimming towards it. It was not clear what the larger police boat – if it was a police boat – was doing. Perhaps it was in the pay of the smugglers, there to ensure no officials interfered with the asylum boat's departure; and when the boat went down, its crew realised they would have a problem explaining their presence, so they left people to drown.

I would never learn if any of Dhanusa's family was found alive. As I was about to ask the second woman's name, someone shouted to her. She ran towards an ambulance that had just arrived. The most unbearable wrenching screams rang out across the clinic grounds. The woman was holding her wet, lifeless son, aged about five. Locals had formed a circle around the woman and were standing, staring at her.

After midday there was a rush of excitement as rescuers began bringing more survivors to shore. They said they had spent the night in life jackets or clinging to debris. An Iranian father wept for joy upon finding his small daughter alive. The girl, apart from crying uncontrollably, was okay. Some reunions were a matter of taking what was left. A teenage girl, whom I'd noticed because she was the Sri Lankan incarnation of my own eldest daughter, ran, arms flailing uncontrollably, when a woman – her mother, aunt or sister, I presumed – was brought from the sea in a wheelchair to the clinic. Joy and loss were being expressed in equal measure. Someone had survived, but someone – a father, a brother – had not.

Another Sri Lankan woman, named Soba, aged twenty-six, told how her husband had already gone ahead by boat to Australia to prepare the way for a new life for herself and two daughters, Marinya and Dhanuya, aged six and two. This man did not yet know that Marinya was dead. Soba told me that after the boat went down, "I asked somebody to help me. I had one hand on a man and one on my baby. And we split. The man held Marinya, but the water was a whirlpool, and Marinya gone. There was too much water in the life jacket and she took it off."

Soba said the life jackets were cheap; they didn't work too well. But amazingly, only thirty or so passengers on the vessel had died.

An Iranian man lifted his shirt and showed me the deep claw marks down his side, where he said a Sri Lankan woman had scratched him as he tried to grab a tube she and others had been clinging onto.

The Sri Lankans and Iranians had come together on the vessel because their respective smugglers had teamed up for this shipment. That likely meant they had reduced overheads by going halves on the cost of the boat, which could be bought for around US$7000–8000, the fee paid by one passenger. This boat was unusual in having no Indonesian crew. The Sri Lankan boat captain was missing, having saved himself. The Iranians were searching the faces of the Sri Lankan survivors as they were brought to the clinic for hot showers, trying to identify crew members. It did not necessarily follow that the Sri Lankans who had assisted the captain were crew, in the proper sense. They may have just been trying to help plug the leak.

By mid-afternoon there was a crowd gathered on the concrete Cidaun jetty watching the fishing boats, which had been commandeered by police, bring in the last of the survivors and bodies. The sea was too rough to do more and the operation ended. I asked Commander Dedy whether he would be investigating the local cops in Cidaun. He asked me why he would do that. I said this was a regular departure point and they must have known about it. The commander did not answer the question. We had a look at the spot up the hill above town where the asylum seekers had been dropped off by vans before setting out on their doomed journey. The residents of this area were frightened, claiming they had seen nothing. I went back to speak to more survivors, particularly the woman I had seen cradling her dead son. But they were all gone.

***

That night we encountered an ambulance transporting the little girl who appeared to be brain-damaged up to the city of Cianjur. We asked the driver if we could stick in its wake and followed it at speed through winding hills to Cianjur hospital, arriving around midnight. They had continued to work on the little girl, whose name was Yasamin, aged three, all through the long drive. She still showed no signs of coming around. Her father, Ahmad, said they had clung to a cabin door all night, without life jackets, and Yasamin had kept going under. We learned the blonde-haired woman who had been in diabetic shock, Fatemah, had also come to this hospital. We spoke to various hospital drivers and learned the Sri Lankan woman who had lost her son had been taken further north to a police hospital in Jakarta, having made the long cross-Java journey nursing his body. We did not know her name but wanted to find her, to learn her story.

Rudd's view was the tragedy was not related to his announcement, nor was it a sign that his policy was not working. "I also said that as soon as it became clear we were making this change the people smugglers would seek to test our resolve by pushing even more at us. So we don't intend to flinch," he told the Nine Network. Tony Abbott announced he would be appointing a three-star general to lead the Coalition's fight against the boats, Operation Sovereign Borders. The message seemed to be that he wanted a more rounded militaristic posture by putting a soldier, rather than a naval officer, in control of what happened on the high seas.

We drove further north to Cisarua, looking for a hotel. We spotted a group of eight or so Iranians who had survived the sinking, trudging along the main road at 1.30a.m. We hailed them down and took them into a little *warung,* or café, to talk. We were surprised to see them there, having assumed they – given the international attention – would have gone into detention or been put in the care of an aid agency. Instead, the police in Cidaun had declared that all fit and able asylum seekers would immediately board police buses and be sent back to Cisarua. They were dumped on the street in the middle of the night.

Among the group of Iranians was a small girl, aged eight, whom they were taking turns carrying. Her name was Hasti and she was the daughter of Fatemah, the woman who had suffered diabetic shock. The little girl was beyond tired. Only eighteen hours earlier, she had been pulled from the sea. When her mother was taken by ambulance to the Cianjur hospital, Hasti was left behind in Cidaun, and this group – some of whom knew her mother – had grabbed Hasti and taken her with them. "We took her with us because we cannot leave her," said Mitt, one of the men. They said they would care for her until they could learn where her mother had been taken. We told them we knew where Fatemah was and were able to put the group in touch with an ambulance driver from the hospital, who said he would coordinate Hasti's return to her mother. But the reunion would never happen. Fatemah's condition did not improve and she died a few nights later. Her body remained unclaimed, and she was buried in a pauper's grave in western Java.

***

We arrived in the Jakarta police hospital the next morning. We knew we were in the right place when we saw the couple, Vinothini and Vimalarasu, who had lost their one-year-old son, Kishanlh. The Disaster Victim Identification Unit that was based there wanted to DNA-match any dead children to their parents. The woman we had been seeking came out of a hospital doorway in a daze. Her name was Selvamalar. She was thirty-nine. Her son's name was Darmithan. He was four.

Selvamalar said the police would not let her see Darmithan. They had taken him from her when they arrived in the ambulance the day before. It was done for practical reasons – the boy had to go into a cold room. "I want my baby, I want to see my baby," she cried. She said she'd dreamed of little else but being with her husband, Balamanokaran, who had escaped to Australia four years earlier on a boat to build a new life in Perth for his wife and then-unborn son, their first child-to-be. He had left Sri Lanka when Selvamalar was five months' pregnant. In Perth, he had cut up photos and made a collage that depicted his family together, as one. He had never met his little son.

Selvamalar told how it had come to this. Late last year she, her brother Rahulan, aged twenty-five, and Darmithan had left their home in Vavuniya, in Sri Lanka's Northern Province. She said her husband faced serious ethnic and political problems as a Tamil. He was living in Perth on a bridging visa. Selvamalar said she'd tried to join her husband through legal means, but was refused a visa. "I don't know why," she said. In mid-November 2012, she set off from Galle, in the south of Sri Lanka, with her son, brother and forty-three other Australia-bound asylum seekers. Each paid the equivalent of around $7200 for passage to Indonesia. She said the engine stopped as they got close to Indonesia on their 2000-kilometre journey. "We were forty-five days in the boat," Selvamalar said. "After twenty-five days, there was no food. Then a ship stopped and give us food. After thirty-six days, we got more food from a New Orient ship. We just floated. On 1 January, we are rescued by a ship and come to Indonesia."

They were taken to Medan, the capital of the North Sumatra province, and put in an overcrowded

Indonesian immigration detention facility with other Sri Lankans, Iranians, Afghans and Burmese. "On 4 April, eight Rohingya persons from Myanmar were murdered by Buddhists in the jail," she said. "I don't know why. They were stabbed. My son saw this. My son is very afraid. We are all very afraid."

After more than three months, the IOM secured their release into community accommodation, but Selvamalar did not want to hang around. She immediately found a smuggler, who arranged for their three-day journey by ferry and bus to Jakarta. By 22 April 2013, the three were in Cisarua. Selvamalar and her brother had no trouble finding the smuggler network. The deal was that Selvamalar and her brother would pay $7200 each. Darmithan, like most small children, would travel free. Selvamalar said she was shown a photo of the boat she would be taking to Australia. "The smugglers say, 'Not a boat, a ship,'" she says. "We saw photo." The photo was of a luxury ocean liner.

It seemed hard to believe that she could accept such a tale, and on this point I did not believe her. Selvamalar said she had never met her smugglers, yet how had she come to see the photo of the ocean liner she would take to Australia? Adding to this, her husband had taken a lousy wooden boat four years ago; surely she knew from his experience that there was no such thing as a luxury ship. But Sri Lankans, I had noticed, were much more cagey about their stories. It did not mean they were less likely to have suffered persecution, perhaps the opposite. They were attuned to the risks of persecution, both at home and on the long run to Australia.

"When we saw the boat, very shocked," Selvamalar said. "But they are saying that this boat will take us to the ship." They motored out to sea for two hours. Selvamalar began to realise there was no big ocean liner; they were on the boat that would take them to Australia. It quickly began taking water through the hull. "We are very afraid," she said. "The boat is in danger." The captain responded to passengers' pleas and turned back for Java, limping on half power for three hours until the boat swamped and quickly began to sink. Selvamalar said that a bigger, more modern boat was just fifty metres from them as people began to struggle and drown. "They are watching our boat," she said. "We say, 'Please help us.' We remove our life jackets and wave. They don't help our rescue. They are watching, watching. We called out, 'Help us, save our life.' They not help."

Selvamalar broke off her narrative. "I want to see my baby. Will you help me?" When I made an inquiry on Selvamalar's behalf, the forensic police politely asked me to keep out of their business.

Selvamalar became separated from her brother (who would survive) and was floating, holding Darmithan. Each had a life jacket, but Selvamalar didn't know how to swim. She didn't want to float further out to sea with her boy. "A man came and took my son," she said. "A Sri Lankan man. He could swim. I gave him my son to take him to safety, to take to land." But Darmithan arrived onshore dead.

What happened? "I don't know, I don't know," she said, bursting into tears again. "On Wednesday I see my son, dead. Very cute boy, very cute boy." She did not know if the man who took her son made it back to shore. She does not know if someone stole her son's life jacket. "My baby was a good dancer, a very good singer," Selvamalar said. "Every day he's saying, 'Mama, I want to see my papa. When will I see my papa? When are we going to Papa?' My baby is always saying to me, 'Don't cry, Mama, don't cry, Mama.' He was very cute, very cute. I wanted him to be a pilot. He was very intelligent, very intelligent."

She didn't know what was to happen. "I don't want to go to Australia," she said. "My life is my baby. My future is my baby. I want my baby. I want to see my baby."

Asked if she had heard of Kevin Rudd, Selvamalar shook her head. "What is that?" She said she knew nothing of the government's new PNG policies, but her smugglers certainly did. Asked what she thought of the smugglers, she said: "They are very cheaters. No life do they understand. Not babies, not pregnant ladies, nothing. They not understand."

THE BOATS SLOW UP

A month later, ten days before the federal election, the pressure was biting hard in Cisarua. Customers were giving up, going home or resigning themselves to long waits for resettlement. They did not want to go to PNG. Kevin Rudd's declaration was working. The boats had slowed to one or two a week.

In Jakarta, we encountered something miraculous: Yasamin, the little girl whom I'd presumed to be brain-damaged, had made a full recovery. She had not been in a damaging coma, as thought, but in some sort of chronic seizure. "I believed she would be like that forever," said her mother, Lale Parnian, twenty-seven, now in IOM-funded accommodation in Jakarta. Yasamin's father, Ahmad, said he knew the risks. He said he would not forgive himself for putting his little daughter on that boat. Yet after coming so close to losing his daughter, Ahmad surprised me: he said he was ready to go alone, again, on a boat.

The little girl Hasti was also now in Jakarta. She still had not been told her mother was dead. Her future was uncertain. I caught up with Mitt, a stockbroker from Tehran, who was among the group looking after Hasti late that night a month before. Mitt had two problems that had sent him on his journey to Australia: he published online advice on Iranian stocks that the government sometimes did not like, which resulted in threatening visits. And his girlfriend was of the wrong religion.

Mitt had got to know Fatemah as they prepared for the boat journey to Australia, and she had told him her story. She had divorced from her husband when Hasti was one, and he had taken no further interest in the child. Fatemah had taken her husband to court to pay child maintenance, but instead the court ruled that under Iranian law any child of a divorced couple belonged in the father's custody. Mitt said part of Fatemah's aim in getting to Australia was to protect Hasti from the risk of being returned to her father, as she grew older and became potentially more useful. Mitt sat with Fatemah and Hasti as the fishermen ferried them to the boat waiting off Cidaun. He remembered Fatemah crying out: "Success!"

Five hours on, the boat was sinking and Fatemah was crying. Mitt was holding Hasti on his knee. He found some life jackets for Fatemah and Hasti. The boat turned around, heading back to Java. "People started to yell that the boat was breaking. We started sinking. Water up to my knees. I see a police boat and one fishing boat. They were watching us. When I go in the water, I have no life jacket. I swim to a person with a life jacket. They punch me. I go to another person, another person. I come to maybe ten, eleven people together, with two tubes. We swim twelve hours until a fishing boat comes and help.

"Before [going on] the boat, Fatemah was not using her injection, because she was worried. She was worried she would feel sick and her levels would be bad. She carried a small plastic box. I said, 'You should use it.' She said, 'After six hours we will reach Christmas Island and then I will do it.' She lost the box at sea. The doctor just put a drip into Fatemah. No insulin."

Once Mitt, Hasti and others were back in Cisarua, their smuggling agent, Naseem, tracked them down. Naseem told Mitt he had moved Fatemah to a private hospital. It was a lie. Naseem had been doing the rounds of the survivors, trying to show concern, in order to put distance between himself and the smuggler boss, Abu Yunis. "Naseem was scared," said Mitt. "He was scared we would go to the police. When we were sinking, we call Naseem. He say, 'Don't worry, I send boat.'" Naseem and Abu Yunis were soon arrested, based on the evidence of survivors. Hasti had been staying with Mitt; he had the money to help her. "She ask, 'Where is my mother?' I tell her she is in hospital, is okay." Hasti was sending messages to her mother on Facebook. Mitt showed me one: "Salaam mama, I am Hasti. I'm with my uncle [Mitt]. I am in café net. My condition is good. When God has you in good condition, I am waiting for you."

When Fatemah died, Mitt said he called one of Fatemah's relatives in Melbourne. When he said Hasti was orphaned, the phone went dead. He sent a

Facebook message to Fatemah's sister, but was blocked. Because Mitt was a single man, he was not deemed a suitable carer for her.

On Hasti's behalf, I rang the office of Tony Burke, Labor's latest, and last, immigration minister, to see if they could assist her. It was not normal for a journalist to do this, it was a line crossed: but Burke's media people were sympathetic to Hasti's story. They said there were ways to circumvent their boss Rudd's claim that no one who came by boat would ever be permitted to settle in Australia; they said they could fast-track her arrival in Australia if she became classified a "person of concern" by the UNHCR. But there were issues. The Australian government, reasonably, needed word from Hasti's father that he'd formally relinquished her guardianship. Mitt was working his contacts, and I was talking to people in Iran on Facebook. Things started to turn ugly. I listened in on a conversation where Mitt accused Hasti's new carers, an Iranian family who had been on the sunken boat, of holding back contact information they had for her father in Iran. Mitt believed they were using Hasti as their meal ticket. They had supposedly won special housing treatment from the IOM because of Hasti's orphan status, and thought it might be possible to use Hasti to expedite their family's resettlement in Australia. Mitt was savage about it. These carers refused to allow me to visit Hasti, so I concluded there was something to it. Then word circled back from Iran that the father was saying he would only renounce custody of Hasti if he was granted Australian citizenship. Then the government changed hands and I lost track of Hasti. So did Mitt.

THE MISLAID INDONESIAN SOLUTION

Selvamalar's boy Darmithan was dead. Kishanlh, the one-year-old son of Vinothini and Vimalarasu, was dead. Hasti had been orphaned, and apparently had become a pawn to be bartered for favourable resettlement outcomes. There was the girl aged twelve, whose body had been lying in the Cidaun hall. Other children whose names were lost at sea were dead. As for Yasamin's father, who still wanted to go ahead alone after nearly losing his daughter at sea, there was a man who did not know how to count his blessings.

It was easy to understand the impatience and the desperation of the asylum seekers, and the risks they took. It was also easy to understand the anxiety of federal politicians, needing results within the short three-year election cycle. You could hear them saying that things were getting better for the Tamils in Sri Lanka, for the Hazaras in Afghanistan, and that Malaysia was a valued friend, and understand why they were saying it, even if it was pernicious horseshit. You could hear the argument about some Iranian asylum seekers being economic migrants and weigh it in the balance. Australia could handle the boat arrivals, even if it was stretching us. We could wonder why crowded Indonesia was big enough to absorb the asylum problem while uncrowded Australia was in a state of strung-out dread. We could accept that a quality bipartisanship on matters of national importance was dead under the current generation of Australian politicians. But if you really wanted to form an opinion on the boats, you could go to YouTube and watch the footage of the 2010 boat crashing into Christmas Island.

The issue did not divide cleanly on political lines. Labor itself was split on the issue: it did not follow that a pro-union Labor member supported kinder border policy. Conservatives were more predictable, having worked themselves into a state where any hint of progressiveness on any issue was seen as a sign of weakness that would expose them to ridicule, or see them excommunicated. Like Malcolm Fraser. Yet no one had a durable answer, not even Howard, under whom most of those who'd been detained on Nauru and Manus Island came to Australia anyway. When Gillard reopened the offshore centres, in the Pacific Solution II, it was no longer proving effective in slowing the boats. Smugglers and passengers knew that time offshore was a short sentence that might have to be served, not a deterrent.

When Rudd took back the leadership from Gillard, three years after she'd taken it from him, he considered asylum seekers one of the key problems of the coming election, particularly among working-class Labor people, who now saw sympathy for boat people as an indulgence of the detached Labor elite. Rudd knew he had to keep the majority onside. "At the beginning we were being punished by the electors because they felt we had not stopped or even slowed the boats down," said Bruce Hawker, Rudd's main strategist. "The polling told us what we'd thought, that there were a lot of misconceptions about boat people, such as that they were living in the lap of luxury and were being treated better than everyone else. Attitudes like that prevailed. There was no appreciable public sympathy for the plight of refugees. They saw them as queue jumpers. Whether that was a convenient way of saying, 'We don't want them,' I didn't think so. It was a more basic anxiety people had about border security. People really believed Howard's line, that 'We will decide who comes to Australia,' very strongly and felt affronted the boats were coming in increasing number and there was no means by which Labor was slowing them. That was being exploited by Abbott, ruthlessly. He was running his famous three-word slogan, Stop the Boats."

The PNG Solution, said Hawker, was Rudd's way of correcting the mistake he'd made in late 2007 of ordering the offshore facilities to shut, without a contingency plan; while at the same time making a genuine attempt to end the deaths at sea. "There's no doubt it was a hard response, but people were dying in big numbers," said Hawker. "I think it was something that he arrived at after a lot of painful reflection on what was actually happening to people. Remember, there were people out there saying he had blood on his hands every time there was a boat going under and people drowned. That was really what drove him more than anything else. Clearly these people smugglers were going to do anything they could to convince these families to get on these leaky boats. Once he was satisfied that the policy just wasn't working, and people were dying in numbers, it was better to come up with a solution while still increasing our intake through the UNHCR. I don't think they anticipated in 2007 the way in which the people smugglers were going to manipulate Labor's policies in the way they did. That was the unforeseen thing in the whole thing. Labor was trying to do the right thing in 2007, and tried to keep it going despite the criticism they were copping, but ultimately his view was people were dying in such numbers we really have to do something."

Rudd's PNG Solution quickly had positive effect on the boats and on Labor voters. "Research by the end of the campaign showed the public's attitude to asylum seekers had changed a lot," said Hawker. "Rudd had been given some recognition for slowing down the boats, to the point where it was no longer registering as a top-line issue in the campaign. He was getting traction on PNG and in the lines he was running against Abbott, that slogans would not cut the mustard. And the public started to respond, but the problem was more complicated. When Abbott said he was going to buy boats [from Indonesian fishermen], Abbott became ludicrous. It was one area where we actually had some success in the lead-up to the election. It was one of the reasons we did better in western Sydney than we would have done. It was working. By the day of the election, it had fallen away as an issue." But by the day of the election, people didn't want Labor.

***

Australia had welcomed the sudden and magnificent democratisation of Indonesia, though it didn't follow that the relationship would get simpler. The dictator, Suharto, had been dependable. Paul Keating eulogised him upon his death in 2008, writing: "Of any figure in the post-World War II period, including any American president, Suharto, by his judgment, goodwill and good sense, had the greatest positive impact on Australia's strategic environment and, hence, on its history."

After a succession of short-term presidents, Suharto was replaced with the steady two-termer, Yudhoyono, who managed many voices in the new political hierarchy. Indonesia was no longer so easy to second-guess when formulating Australian foreign policy. Yet Yudhoyono was prepared sometimes to aggravate his senior ministers by treating Australia as a valued friend. He had assisted Rudd, but that did not extend to giving Australia what it really wanted, which was for Indonesia to stop the boats at sea and to create a massive asylum-and-refugee sorting shed. Indonesia knew exactly how such a processing centre might work, having pushed 250,000 Indochinese refugees through its camp on Galang Island between 1979 and 1996. Created under Suharto – who was persuaded by Western powers, including Australia under Malcolm Fraser, to set up a regional centre to warehouse the Indochinese fleeing communism – it was built and managed by Suharto's cronies and became its own human-rights fiasco, with riots, suicides, filthy conditions, epidemics, complaints of rape against the guards and tortuously slow resettlement processing by the UNHCR. Indonesia's view, at the time of its closure, was: never again.

For Indonesia to manage another regional scheme, for Australia's benefit, there were considerable practical obstacles, even before going into the deeper social problems that would need to be overcome. As Dave McRae, until recently a research fellow at the Lowy Institute for International Policy's East Asia Program, put it: "Agreeing to processing would be akin to taking back people who had already left ... If they're found not to be refugees, would Indonesia be able to repatriate them to their countries of origin? If they are refugees, will another country definitely accept them for resettlement, given the general shortage of resettlement places? To date, boat departures have largely allowed Indonesia to bypass these issues."

Australian diplomats had never packaged up a comprehensive plan for an Indonesian Solution; or, if such a plan was ever devised and presented to Jakarta, the detail of it never reached the ears of the most informed Australian academics or journalists. Nor did it serve the interests of Australian politicians to run through the exhaustive list of why Australia did not pursue, at high diplomatic level, such a scheme, because the answers were too raw to be ventilated. It fell to academics, such as Professor Tim Lindsey, director of the Asian Law Centre at Melbourne University, to explain some of Indonesia's more deeply held objections. His points could be summarised like this: Indonesia's leaders resented the view that they should be doing more to stop the boats, because asylum seekers were only in Indonesia to get to Australia; they saw it as hypocritical that we would not accept asylum seekers, yet expected they should; they resented our Fortress Australia mindset; they viewed the Afghanistan and Iraq wars, which Indonesia did not support, as having created an asylum problem within Indonesia; and furthermore, Lindsey argued, Indonesia was more interested in building its diplomatic ties elsewhere and didn't see great political value in assisting Australia.

Despite all this, Lindsey's view, based on discussions with his high-level contacts in Jakarta, was that Indonesia might have been open to coordinating a regional solution – at the right price. "Indonesia has been waiting a long time for a serious proposal that would put it front-and-centre of a regional solution," he said. "Everything else has been a distraction. But Indonesia would not enter into such an arrangement lightly or quickly. There would need to be serious inducements made. Significant money and resources need to be offered." Yet such an offer had never come. Perhaps the price – which would presumably include ships and onshore facilities – was too high. And now that Yudhoyono was completing his second and final presidential term, due to expire in mid-2014, that opportunity had slipped away.

Lindsey regarded my personal view that the Australian public had in the last decade developed a warmer and more sophisticated understanding of Indonesia as naive; and, after being pointed to the polling and surveys, I concluded he was right. As Indonesia democratised, Australians had instead viewed Indonesia as an increased threat, accompanied by acute ignorance about the country. DFAT's 2013 survey showed that only 70 per cent of Australians knew that Bali was part of Indonesia. In fact, half of those aged between eighteen and twenty-four – the crowd that went there most often – thought Bali was a country in its own right, or part of another country, or they didn't know. Our views were informed not by what should have been the celebration of Indonesia's emergence from the Suharto years, but by the 2002 and 2005 Bali bombings, Abu Bakar Bashir, the Australian embassy bombing in Jakarta, the JW Marriott and Ritz-Carlton bombings, the Bali Nine, Schapelle Corby, the live cattle trade, influenza outbreaks, the 2004 tsunami and earthquakes. It was a bad place, once you left the main drag of crowded Kuta – where the memory of 12 October 2002 had been drowned with Bintang and shooters.

Australians followed the relationship through a series of supposedly difficult incidents, as though a constant state of mild crisis was necessary to sharing the neighbourhood. The brinkmanship between Indonesia and Australia had not since *konfrontasi* led to armed encounters – except for a minor few unforeseen border skirmishes with departing rogue elements in the carefully stage-managed East Timor liberation of 1999. Instead the two countries acted as dogs marking out territory that was wholly uncontested. We each pissed on our own trees. We had no territorial disputes, and there was no chance we would do for West Papua what we had done for East Timor. The notion of conflict with Indonesia was unthinkable to anyone half-abreast of the realities, yet we could not seem to cross the line to full friendship. "It's our natural ally in the region, and we're the only two multi-party democracies in the region," Lindsey said. "We are natural partners. Government-to-government relations have been warm, close and enthusiastic, but that's not true for the public. It loathes and fears Indonesia. The knee-jerk reaction drives governments to follow the popular, not the government, view. That is why there is fragility in the relationship, because the Australian public is grossly misinformed."

Those Australians who believed they lived in the most desirable country in the world, one that Indonesia was itching to get its hands on, overlooked an important point: none of the asylum seekers heading south in boats was Indonesian, apart from a handful of West Papuans who had never considered themselves part of that country. Indonesians had no desire to live in

Australia. This was backed by a telling statistic: young Indonesians on student visas were among the groups *least* likely to overstay and attempt to take up residency.

The popular Australian view of Indonesia as an aggressive militaristic state, dominated by Islamic hardliners, was erroneous. Indonesia was now a fully open society, its army back in barracks, its media and academics outspoken; it had no plans to acquire any other country's territory, and the influence of Islamic political parties had declined to the lowest levels since the first post-Suharto elections. With Australia's help, Jemaah Islamiyah had been tracked down and smashed, with Indonesia showing zero tolerance for the terrorism that had wrought such heartache in *both* countries. There would still be extremists; there always would. But the moderation and tolerance exhibited by the world's largest Islamic country was remarkable to behold.

In the Suharto obituary, Keating gave his view on the reasons Australia had issues with Indonesia: "So why have Australians regarded Indonesia so suspiciously, especially over the past quarter-century, when it is evident that Indonesia has been at the fulcrum of our strategic stability? Unfortunately, I think the answer is Timor and the wilful reporting of Indonesian affairs in Australia by the Australian media, in the main the Fairfax press and the ABC." Keating considered Australia's response to the murder of five Australian journalists at Balibo by Indonesians a petulant overreaction. He said the reporters had been sent to East Timor by irresponsible media proprietors, and ought not have been reporting the invasion at all.

Whatever Keating's view on the telling of history, one thing was clear from his hagiographic assessment of Suharto: he had no concept of how ordinary non-political Indonesians lived in abject terror of the small military posts that occupied every small town and village that existed during the long dictatorship. He understood Indonesia strictly from the top down, blind to the fears of ordinary people, or their strong desire to be able to breathe out and talk openly without fear of punitive visits. In this could be found the reason for Indonesia's democratisation, but it lay beyond Keating's powers of conception.

It might have been expected that an anti-communist country would be more naturally allied to a Coalition government than to an Australian Labor Party leader, yet Keating and Rudd formed the closest ties with Indonesia. For his part, Howard seemed to extract value from regarding Indonesia as a threat. No one pissed on his own tree quite like Howard. There were many things he understood well: he read the prevailing national moods better than anyone. But other countries and cultures – including Australian indigenous culture – were not among them. Australians were caught between Keating's support of despotism and Howard's inclination to insularity. It would take Rudd and Yudhoyono finally to start getting the balance right.

Yudhoyono, in his address to the Australian parliament in 2010, said he understood that many Australians held misplaced views about his country, fearing it as a breeding ground for extremism. Likewise, he said, Indonesians held outdated views on Australia as a defiant White Australia outpost. He said we all needed to get over the "preposterous mental caricatures" we held of each other. Yudhoyono had gone straight to the core of the issues in an unusually candid act of statesmanship that, at its heart, kindly suggested we may as well get over the paternalism because Indonesia had overtaken Australia in terms of global significance. Soon enough, it would not need our money. Yudhoyono, unaware that a few months earlier his good friend Rudd had bugged his phone, came to Australia with a promise to criminalise people-smuggling, which was warmly received. This small offering also showed how far we were from the Indonesian Solution we should have been pursuing all along. But he brought to Canberra some worthwhile words: "We are equal stakeholders in a common future with much to gain if we get this relationship right, and much to lose if we get it wrong." With Indonesia on track to become one of the world's top ten economies within fifteen years, and in the top five by 2050, it followed that we needed to think about getting on board with the emerging regional superpower if we were not to leave ourselves stranded at the bottom of the world.

Our expertise in the hunt for terrorists had, we were told, produced remarkable results. But this was also taken by the Australian audience as confirmation that Indonesia was a terror-state. We did not seem to appreciate how Indonesia tended to fall on the side of the West, and how through its ownership of airspace and sea-lanes Indonesia could provide Australia's greatest shield against attack. "That's why it's critical to have a relationship," said Lindsey. "And Indonesia has shown if we can't work in partnership they'll just cut us off. The impact would be small for them and huge for us. Our military strategy would be in shreds, our capacity to stop boats would be in shreds. Our aid programs would be cut, ending our access and influence, and we would ultimately lose access to new markets, and our access to one of the world's rising powers would end. By 2050, they might be completely uninterested in us. It might not matter in a year, but it would in five or ten. Indonesia has been a friendly agent that has got us into the regional architecture (meaning it has assisted us with introductions across Southeast Asia). It's been critical. If our relationship is damaged, so too is our access to the region and we will end up isolated.

"We are the junior partner. We may not like it, but we need to think about what will make ourselves useful and relevant to Indonesia. Yudhoyono really likes Australia – or, he did. He was genuinely interested. He stood up for us." Australian spying and wire-tapping saw small rent-a-crowds forming outside our embassy in Jakarta and burning flags, but that was not the problem. It was aggravating the Indonesian leadership – and some of the current political elite, who had studied in Australia and understood us well, were becoming the most outspoken against us. They knew their country was rising, and that our attitudes were stifling us.

We had helped hunt terrorists, but we needed more shared interests. The most obvious one to exploit was the rise of China. Rudd, who under Gillard became both foreign minister and then foreign minister-in-exile, often gave lectures to think-tanks, particularly in the US, advising that China was a merchant colonist, not an invader; that its truest ambition was to raise the living standards of its own people, rather than to start wars. Yet Indonesia remained deeply anxious about China, as did the US. Australia liked to appear unworried, because it did not want to offend our most important trade customer. But it was clear where we would stand as the US began its slow pivot towards Asia and commenced annual joint military exercises with Indonesia. If the US filed Rudd's views under "Whatever," Rudd was not telling Indonesia anything it did not already know: it saw itself as having been steadily undermined for decades by Chinese-Indonesians, who were greatly overrepresented in the country's economy. Beijing, as well, was threatening Indonesia's gas interests in the South China Sea; and Indonesia feared the Chinese navy as a direct threat. For a would-be regional superpower,

Tim Lindsey noted, Indonesia's navy was seriously underpowered: "On their own estimate, they could get twenty-five functional naval ships in the water at any one time, over 17,400 islands."

The sea was Indonesia's sorest point, because it was its weakest point. It followed it would become furious at any suggestion of any incursion on its sovereignty, because it could do very little to police its own waters. It was never going to permit Australian naval boats untrammelled access to patrol its coastline to stop boats. It had the controlling interest in arguably the most important strategic and economic shipping lane in the world, the Strait of Malacca, and its sensitivities could be seen in its refusal to let the US naval ships guard American merchant vessels using the strait from piracy. Yet it was looking for friends to assist more broadly with its security. It was finding them in Washington DC and Delhi, even though we threw more than half a billion dollars at Indonesia every year, most of it going on education, governance, economic development and health. It was, you were told, an aid program of extraordinary social penetration, which in turn gave us great access to government. Most Indonesians knew nothing about it; Australians, if they did, resented it.

We did, in fact, treat Indonesia as our most important relationship. But that was Rudd's, and Gillard's, and Labor's problem: they were never able to sell a story.

Rudd understood that Indonesia mattered most. John Howard's liberation of East Timor in 1999 – which Labor would never have initiated – brought an ironic consequence: East Timor had invited Beijing down to Dili, breaking the link in the archipelago chain and weakening the Indonesian shield. Indonesia, remarkably, had put Timor behind it and moved on; while we were left with a slightly antagonistic East Timor, under the sulking Xanana Gusmão. Rudd ended direct aid to China and India and greatly increased aid to Indonesia, reflecting the reality that we needed Indonesia more than it needed us. Yet by late 2013 and across into 2014, Australia–Indonesia relations were at their lowest point since 1999. Our shared problem of asylum seekers could have been the basis for strong regional cooperation. Instead, Abbott was not just testing Indonesia's sensitivities on its sovereignty by threatening to turn or tow back the boats – he was actually doing this.

SENDING THEM BACK

Three weeks after winning government, Abbott was in Indonesia, on his first overseas visit, where he apologised to Yudhoyono for the election campaign, saying Australian politicians (meaning himself and Scott Morrison) should have "said less and done more" in criticising Indonesia for the boats that had come our way. And he heard some very gracious and reassuring words from Yudhoyono. "Australia and Indonesia are both victims of people smugglers," the president said. "A lot of people from other countries, from the Middle East and a lot of other countries, have put a lot of pressure on Indonesia. A group of these people wish to continue to Australia, and this puts pressure on Indonesia. We would like to work together with Australia, with effective cooperation and good cooperation. There needs to be bilateral cooperation between Australia and Indonesia. We will continue to grow to overcome this issue." They were his last kind words to Australia.

The nature of the cooperation was not specified. Abbott, a few days later, was in Bali for the Asia-Pacific Economic Cooperation summit, where he met the Malaysian prime minister, Najib Tun Razak, and explained that he and his colleagues had never meant anything they said about Malaysia being an appalling human-rights violator. That had been non-core sledging. "Our criticism was never of Malaysia, it was of the former government," he said after the meeting with Razak. "I guess you might say that, in my own way, I offered an apology because I appreciate this was a difficult situation for Malaysia, and it was only in that difficult situation because, in its own way, it had tried to help out a friend."

Then Abbott was in Perth, addressing the WA Liberal Party State Council, providing no clues on how the new cooperation with Indonesia might work but reiterating the sovereignty line. It always sounded like a friendly warning. "This is an issue of sovereignty for us, and that's very important," Abbott said. "When I was up in Jakarta a few weeks ago, I was able to tell President Yudhoyono, a very good friend of our country, an outstanding President of Indonesia, I was able to tell him that we utterly, totally, completely respected Indonesian sovereignty and if any boat ever set out from Australia to Indonesia to enter that country illegally, we would do our damndest to stop it. We would do our damndest to stop it and I think he understood that our sovereignty is just as important to us as their sovereignty is to them. We have good relations with Indonesia, good and improving relations with Indonesia, but we will stop these boats. We will stop these boats. In any test of will between the Australian government and the people smugglers, we will and we must prevail. But, friends, I said that my first trip as prime minister would be to Jakarta, and it was, and our foreign policy now has a Jakarta, not a Geneva focus, as it should."

"Geneva" was presumably Abbott's reference to the United Nations-loving, jet-setting Rudd. Abbott's claim that his government viewed Jakarta as Australia's most important relationship was welcome, but only if it was true. It seemed that Abbott was saying the solution was very simple: it was up to Indonesia, not Australia, to stop the boats.

Then came the revelation of the bugging of the president's and first lady's phones, leading Indonesia to suspend joint military exercises and any cooperation on the boats. The eavesdropping had come just after the JW Marriott and Ritz-Carlton suicide bombings in Jakarta, which killed three Australians. It may have been an attempt to find out what Yudhoyono knew, but according to the *Australian*' s Cameron Stewart the reason for the 2009 intrusion was an attempt by the Australian Signals Directorate – presumably with the blessing of Rudd – to keep abreast of developments in a Hillary Clinton-style political succession plan supposedly being hatched by Yudhoyono's wife, Kristiani Herawati. Yudhoyono was incensed. It was left to the Abbott government to try to minimise the damage.

Scott Morrison adopted a strategy of holding lengthy weekly briefings that imparted no operational information, especially on whether Australia was turning or towing back the boats. After a boat sank off Java in early October, former immigration minister Amanda Vanstone had written a pestilential piece for the *Age,* barracking for Morrison's information blackout.

She claimed the media and people smugglers were a team. "Their modus operandi is to get as many sad stories associated with asylum seekers into the Australian media as possible," she wrote. "They want to press our sympathy button until we can't stand it anymore." She resented the media for interviewing the survivors of that particular sinking. Advocating the non-reporting of the asylum issue from any but the Coalition government's perspective, she considered reporters had shown sympathy and bias by shoving microphones in the faces of a few survivors and asking them what had happened. Who knows what would have emerged if she'd been given another few hundred words to develop her theories: perhaps accusations of treason for anyone who questioned government policy.

One solution would have been for the *Age* to deny Vanstone any column space, but that was how government, not media, worked. Intermittent word was drifting out that conditions were not so good on Manus Island, Christmas Island, at Curtin Detention Centre or on Nauru, from where Iranian asylum seeker Elena Abbasi sent me an email in November: "we are not having enough water for buthroom also that is only 5 minutes. we are leaving in tents and is very hot all the time. and evry body in here up very ungry even the child and is happening alot of fights, and there is no doctor in here and so many of people that they are here they need doctor." It did not need Vanstone to see that this skerrick of information was not enough for a "sympathetic" story. There was little reliable information to form a view on what was really happening in the camps.

Four Corners reported a former Manus Island doctor, John Valentine, as saying that medical supplies were in desperately short supply and despite repeated requests for routine items – such as oxygen – they did not arrive. The *Guardian Australia* released a report from fifteen doctors attending to asylum seekers on Christmas Island, complaining conditions were not adequate to treat children, pregnant women or people with disabilities. It also said that passengers arrived covered in their own faeces and urine after long, cramped boat journeys and were suffering from a condition known as "boat rash." What measures the authorities might have taken to ensure they arrived in better condition was not expressed. However, the doctors also complained that "basic medical stocks are low; drugs requested by doctors are not provided; long delays in transferring patients to mainland hospitals are leading to risks of 'life-threatening deterioration.'" The report, which the doctors submitted to their employer, International Health and Medical Services, in November, was vague on how long this had been going on, but the doctors were said to have been complaining about the issues "for some time." In other words, the situation had existed under Labor.

For the Persian Iranians who were now in offshore facilities or on bridging visas, their decision to take the boats was not resulting in the outcomes they wanted. They were failing at every stage of the application process. What this meant was that their numbers, both in detention centres and on bridging visas in the community, had grown steadily throughout 2012 and 2013. Iran refused to accept involuntary returns, meaning they could not be forced home.

An Immigration source provided me with an extreme assessment of the Persians, which gave some clues to the department's defensive mindset: "What happens is they are the most belligerent, testy and high-expectation cohort in the whole network. They are educated, skilled, bilingual, they've generally made the trip within a week or ten days, and they have been promised an outcome. When they get to Christmas Island, they are treated no differently. They are interviewed and invariably they are not found to engage our protection obligations. But the system is such that there are thousands of people who haven't been formally processed. Most Iranians are knocked back, though some have bona fides. With those who are knocked back, it's because their reason for selecting Australia is because they've had a gutful of the conservative mullahs. We're now at a position where there are 6000–8000 Iranians who are unlikely to get an outcome. No Western government has a returns agreement with Tehran for involuntary returns. Tehran will not take them back.

"This is intractable. This is not Tiananmen Square. The Iranians have led the riots at Christmas Island and Nauru. They are the most violent standover people. They throw their weight around and they'll be tough to move out. Even if they did word themselves up (on claims of persecution), it's hard for a well-dressed bejewelled person without scars and without identifiable injuries to claim persecution. They're not activists, they're not Christians. It doesn't stack up, no matter how plush the story is. But they're pretty upfront. They want freedom. 'A chance for our children.'

"If some sought to come the lawful way, we would reach out to them. But the Iranian diaspora in Australia does not want a bar of them. The generation of Iranians that are here fled the overthrow of the Shah or came with skilled migration. Those Iranians are highly regarded.

"But we are stuck with this cohort. They have no right to remain in Australia, but Tehran will not allow them back. This is going to be a hard nut to crack. We need to come to some arrangement with Tehran to return these people. Because, in their minds, they're almost here."

There had been longstanding simmering resentment from immigration officers, who knocked back most applications for protection visas at the first instance (wherever people were from), only to find their decisions overturned by lawyers working for the Refugee Review Tribunal, also known as the independent merits review process. Said the Immigration source: "It's been systemic that the RRT has been antagonistic to department decision-making. When you look at how many decisions are being overturned, is it any wonder they take the boats?"

Lawyer David Manne, who'd beaten the government on Malaysia, said the reason why so many Immigration decisions were overturned was because officers, who were not lawyers, had systemically failed to apply proper legal principles when considering cases. He said the department's work was of such low competence that the RRT had no choice but to overrule. However, with the Persian-Iranian cohort, fewer Immigration decisions were being overturned.

By February, things were going bad on Manus Island, where some 1340 single men were housed in shipping containers in the processing centre, located within the Lombrum naval base. Some had been on Manus for five months or more. Their claims had not begun to be processed and they were starting to lose patience. On Sunday the 16th, after two weeks of mild freedom-chanting and demands for answers as to what was to become of them, the situation quickly deteriorated. In the morning, according to islander sources and witnesses, various aggrieved asylum-seeker nation groups within the camp sent their representatives to meet with officers from Immigration, its security contractor G4S (which employed locals and other PNG nationals as unarmed guards inside the compound) and the Salvation Army. They wanted to know when their claims would begin to be processed; and sought clear word of whether they would be able to apply to settle in PNG or another country if found to be refugees. They set a deadline for an answer of 4p.m. that same day. It was not known what leverage they brought to the table to make such a demand, unless it was threats of upheaval. It seems they were accommodated in this regard: an answer came back from Canberra, on deadline, that some of them might have to wait four full years before their claims would be processed. Another version was that they were told things had changed and they would never be allowed to settle even in PNG, though Scott Morrison would deny they were ever given such a message. Yet Morrison would later confirm that the Manus deal, set up by Rudd, was poor on detail, and that PNG had no firm measures in place on taking refugees.

That night, a group of detainees pushed down a gate but were repelled back inside the compound by G4S guards, while their Australian bosses looked on. A mobile squad of heavily armed riot police from the Highlands, known as PNG's most ruthless response cops, and tasked with guarding the outer perimeter of the facility, also stood looking on with dogs and guns. The protest eventually settled, but the following night trouble intensified as hundreds of detainees raged around two of the centre's compounds, breaking their beds into weapons, grabbing fire extinguishers, rocks and whatever they could find. Local eyewitnesses told me that the asylum seekers had been taunting the G4S guards and the riot squad police, yelling,

"Fuck PNG," "You are an AIDS country," and "We'll fuck your wives and fuck your sisters." This went down very badly with both groups of guards, none of whom had the training to handle such confrontations. That night they went *inside* the compound and cracked heads, killing one man, a 23-year-old Iranian Kurd named Reza Barati, firing rounds and belting the hell out of seventy-seven others. Later I saw three of the protesters as they were being taken off Manus Island, all bearing double black eyes and looking quite frightened. It was not clear where they were going, because immigration officers and G4S guards would not let us talk to them. As for Barati, there were several versions of how he died, though there was no question he'd had his skull caved in. He had been observed regularly doing weights and boxing training at the centre and was described by locals as the most aggressive and vocally offensive of the riot leaders. He was either stomped in the head while on the ground or repeatedly slammed in the head with a riot shield or length of wood. Whether it was G4S or the Papuan riot police was not clear. It was said – though the information was not exactly reliable given there was a battle going on involving hundreds – that Barati had been shaping up and punching on harder than anyone and that he'd hospitalised at least one G4S guard, though others described him as a "gentle giant."

Locals who lived within the Lombrum base had also entered the compound at the request of the guards to help put the protesters down. They didn't need much encouragement after hearing the insults the asylum seekers had been throwing around. One of those who went in said they had armed themselves with iron bars. This man saw Barati being taken away by medics and told me: "His skull was crushed and his neck was broken, but I don't know how." PNG and Australia announced they would hold separate inquiries. Barati had left Java on 24 July, five days after Rudd's PNG edict. He represented the last big push of boats to Australia. And he had made it to Christmas Island, but no closer to Australia.

I drove up to the detention facility and – before being chased away by riot police – was able to get a good look at it, and the sorry post-riot asylum seekers wandering about, hanging out their washing and talking in small groups. What seemed most incongruous was how low-key the centre's security was: there was no barbed or razor wire on the compound, just standard cyclone fences. Any detainee could have jumped the fence, anytime, not that there was anywhere an escapee could go. The island itself was the prison. But that was the point of offshore detention: it was about sending a message to all others thinking of coming down to Australia that they would never know the comfort of the mainland.

I found that locals strongly supported the presence of the detention centre on their island, an otherwise starved outpost north of the mainland in the Bismarck Sea. It meant lots of jobs. Though there had been a centre under Howard's Pacific Solution I, it was much smaller; and, outside the Lombrum base, closer to the main township, work was underway to build a large open centre to hold families whose refugee claims had been approved and who were awaiting resettlement. Australian building contractors were long-renting hotel rooms and lodges and the place was beginning to boom as locals benefited from subcontracts or straight employment. There was also indignation, because when Rudd did the original deal with Peter O'Neill, a "Manus Package" had been promised, including the upgrading of schools, roads and a new airport. None of this had so far arrived, but O'Neill was starting to spend the Australian government's money elsewhere in PNG.

The question about the Manus and Nauru facilities was who held responsibility when things went wrong, as they had on both islands. Australia paid for everything, including for security, but one Australian official who came in from Moresby to inspect the Manus carnage gave his position: "This is not an Australian facility. This is wholly owned and run by Papua New Guinea. It's not our facility." That was a nice handball, but it hardly sounded right. How could you create something, determine who won contracts, control it, manage it, run it, have Australian immigration officials walking around a foreign country telling Australian journalists not to take photos in public places, and then say you had nothing to do with it? If the G4S guards and the riot police were in foul moods, chasing us away when they could, you could understand this: someone was going to answer for the way the riot was handled, and Barati's death was possibly a murder, given that the guards had gone in to deal with him and the others rather than tackling them outside on public land. They were protecting each other's backs.

I did not share the view of asylum-advocacy groups that Morrison should resign over Barati's death. This centre was owned by Howard, Gillard, Rudd *and* Abbott. Yes, it happened under Morrison's watch, but it could have happened under any immigration minister's watch. Labor had set this camp up, and had it won the election there was no reason to think that PNG would have moved any faster to process the detainees' claims. The argument that Morrison or the Coalition had blood on their hands epitomised the inexplicable pro-asylum view that Labor was always more forgivable, or somehow more humane, than the other side. Both parties had identical policies, apart from the boat turn-backs. The real problem with the centre's security was that it was too weak. It had been conceived of as a processing centre, not a prison. The fact is the detainees took advantage of the situation on Manus. They were certainly frustrated, and both Australia and PNG were remiss not to expect or plan for trouble. If you were going house close on 1400 pent-up men, you needed to get security right. You could not, you would think, subcontract a government's ideology to a group like G4S, said to be the largest private security firm in the world but one with a poor reputation (see its London Olympics fiasco) and which employed half-trained locals on low wages. Morrison agreed that G4S had served the centre poorly. It was already on the way out, having failed to have its contract renewed, but he was rushing its staff out of the centre, replaced by Transfield, who had subcontracted guarding the Manus camp to a new team from Wilson Security, a group most Australians associated with running carparks.

***

Abbott had adopted Rudd's position on boat arrivals. "This government will never allow people who come here illegally by boat to gain permanent residency in Australia," Abbott said in December. And he had gone one significant step beyond. In mid-January, the commander of Operation Sovereign Borders, Lieutenant General Angus Campbell, reported that no asylum seekers had come ashore in Australia during the last five weeks. That was because they were being turned back. The best guess, by mid-January (by when Minister Morrison had stopped the public briefings), was that the Coalition government had nudged five boats back towards Indonesia since the September election, but that was neither confirmed nor denied. Indonesia's foreign minister, Marty Natalegawa, said the Australian government's purchase of powered lifeboats, which were being used to transfer asylum seekers from dodgy boats and send them back to

Indonesia, had changed the nature of the problem and was "a slippery slope." Mahfudz Siddiq, chairman of Indonesia's Foreign Affairs Commission, explained that this was now "a smuggling operation, legalised by the Australian government."

Abbott and Morrison had kept their word, which was to repeat the John Howard experience. They had also overlooked one of Howard's most winning traits, being that he would always dutifully show up and explain his position, for better or worse, in the midst of the deepest political storm. Howard had turned back seven boats, in a time when there were many arrivals; and, as Alexander Downer wrote last year in the *Advertiser,* this measure – along with offshore processing and temporary protection visas – had more or less stopped the flow. Abbott was turning them back in a time of few boats. His government had also shown that with its zero boat tolerance it was prepared to test the limits of Indonesian forbearance. This was a total sovereign stand-off. Scott Morrison apologised to Indonesia after Australian Border Protection Command vessels several times entered Indonesian waters for reasons Morrison would not disclose, but it was likely on push-back or tow-back operations. Border Protection Command was off the leash. Or had misplaced their GPS. With an unknown incoming president due by mid-year – and none of the likely candidates appearing likely to share Yudhoyono's now-depleted enthusiasms for Australia – it felt as if dark times were ahead.

Although Yudhoyono accepted a letter of explanation from Abbott on the phone tapping, Indonesia had suspended cooperation on people smuggling, military exercises and intelligence sharing. These would remain suspended until the president and Abbott signed off on a "six-step roadmap." The roadmap, proposed by Indonesia, was agreed to by Foreign Minister Julie Bishop after meeting Foreign Minister Natalegawa. It was not a list of specific demands but a drawn-out timetable for a series of meetings to negotiate protocols on bilateral conduct (which really meant Australia's conduct). Once that was done, possibly by late 2014, Australia would need to sign another code of ethics on spying. We had entered a period of slow freeze, yet there was a victory of sorts: Cisarua was almost cleaned out of asylum seekers. The Iranians had mostly gone home or were in detention centres scattered across the archipelago, awaiting formal resettlement. A veteran failed Afghan asylum seeker, Ali Abbas Josh, thirty-five, who'd been repelled after trying to make Australia by boat under John Howard, and had come back last year for another try, said hope was gone in Cisarua. "We agree the way to Australia has been closed," he said. "We accept that you have closed the way, that you won't take us if we come by boat."

Australia's position had become difficult to follow. On the one hand, our foreign policy was to strengthen ties with Indonesia. Yet Abbott, as commander-in-chief, was unilaterally sending back the boats. It was suggested by one commentator, Ross Taylor, the chairman of the WA-based Indonesia Institute, that Indonesia quietly saw itself as the beneficiary of the turn-back policy, because it was helping solve its own asylum-seeker problems. Taylor argued we needed to manage the relationship with great care, but said that at a deeper level, "Indonesia and Australia need each other." This seemed to mirror the thinking in Canberra. If so, the view had rapidly become outdated. Indonesia, in case no one had noticed, had set Australia to one side. An intelligence officer on the coast told me that Java's smuggling hotspots were now being flooded with spies in an attempt to expose and arrest members of the police and military who were obviously heavily involved in helping smugglers move passengers to the coast and onto boats. Indonesia finally wanted to stop the boats: not to help Australia but – as I guessed it, given cooperation was suspended – to give it less reason to have anything to do with us.

Labor had shown that confusion and inconsistency could not be sold to a domestic audience as policy. As for Indonesia, it did not have a preference as to whether Australia had a Labor or a Liberal-National government. It was the leader that mattered to them. Even before arriving in office, Abbott had wilfully set course for difficulties with Indonesia by insisting on the turn-backs. It appeared he had no longer view on how it would play out, treating it as a short-course triathlon. Turning back boats was good campaign politics but poor long-term policy.

In late January, back in Ujung Genteng on the south coast of Java, I found a fisherman who had taken some photos on his phone of a strange orange vessel that had come ashore at Cikepuh, by a remote forestry reserve. This would serve as the first close-up photographic evidence of the lifeboats Tony Abbott was sending back to Indonesia. A week after that, another one came ashore on the central Java coast. The naval officers in Ujung Genteng who seized and impounded the lifeboat took no issue with Australia sending people back to Indonesia. They could sympathise with the sovereignty argument, so it followed that they did not appreciate the Australian naval vessel that had entered its waters on a push-back mission. If the push-backs were brutal, the lifeboats – designed to stop asylum seekers demanding rescue after scuttling their wooden boats – were ingenious. But Abbott, having inherited the phone-spying scandal that resulted in suspended cooperation, had in a sense been licensed by Indonesia to act unilaterally by sending back the boats; if it refused to have anything to do with Australia, how could it complain? Indonesia had therefore enabled Abbott to take the role of silent strongman, though this did not appear to be an act of deference or submission. It felt, instead, that Indonesia was turning away.

The sight of a beached lifeboat might have been startling, yet what came next was the real surprise: in early February, Scott Morrison was in Malaysia, doing business with the government that he had described as a ruthless abuser of human rights and which Abbott – and a chorus of senior Coalition members – had described as cruel to asylum seekers. Morrison, photographed at the helm of a Malaysian interceptor vessel in the Strait of Malacca, said Malaysia would be getting two ex-Customs boats to help it police its waters. He talked of new cooperation on asylum seekers and smugglers. And Malaysia was suddenly expressing interest in catching people island-hopping back to Malaysia after failing to catch boats to Australia from Indonesia – the same people Malaysia had allowed to breach Indonesian sovereignty in the first place.

So much for Abbott's "Jakarta focus" – this looked more like the middle finger. Instead of working slowly to rebuild what was said to be our most important relationship, we had – according to Morrison – put Kuala Lumpur ahead of Jakarta as a "key partner in regional and bilateral efforts against people smuggling." Australia and Indonesia remained too distrustful of each other, and most of that distrust was generated in Canberra. This was evidenced by the willingness to listen in on a good friend's phone and to treat one of the world's great nations as a sideshow town off an exit ramp on the road to somewhere better. If you tried explaining to a child the difficulties we had with

Indonesia, a country that did not threaten us or seek to make our lives more difficult, and had experienced among the most peaceful democratic revolutions of modern times, you'd struggle.

On my most recent trip to Indonesia, I noticed a big street poster in central Jakarta announcing Komodo 2014, a multilateral naval exercise hosted by Indonesia. The flags of all major regional and non-regional "allies" were displayed. Except for Australia's. It was sad.

If the deepest fear of Canberra was that one day Indonesia would stand up as a rich economy with a formidable military, that was many decades away. But China was already there. In early February, the Lowy Institute's Rory Medcalf reported that a Chinese taskforce of three warships had entered the Sunda Strait to conduct combat exercises "somewhere between Indonesia and Christmas Island."

"This is the first substantial Chinese military exercise in the eastern part of the Indian Ocean and in Australia's maritime approaches," Medcalf wrote.

> It seems also to be the first time a Chinese taskforce has transited the Sunda and Lombok straits as alternatives to the Malacca Strait. With this decidedly Indo-Pacific foray, China is sending many signals, deliberately or not. One is about its ability and ambition to project force through and beyond the South China Sea. Another is its wish to be seen to be interested in protecting its

> commercial sea lanes into the Indian Ocean. A third is that the People's Liberation Army-Navy will go where it wants when it wants, without necessarily consulting or forewarning local powers.

Such unannounced visits showed why we needed to be on good terms with Indonesia. When US secretary of state John Kerry dropped by Jakarta in mid-February, Marty Natalegawa briefed him on what he considered Australia's bad manners over the boats. It would be interesting to know what the US thought about all of this – whether it was anxious that Australia was too dismissive of Indonesia, a country it greatly valued. But that would have to wait for another Edward Snowden-type classified-file drop.

Something else had been lost, and it was exemplified in the attacks on the ABC for daring to report allegations that Border Protection Command had burned the hands of three asylum seekers who'd been turned back to Indonesia. It was now deemed unacceptable and unpatriotic to test such a claim. Senator David Johnston said of the Somali man who made the allegation: "He's not even Australian." Abbott, who has always enjoyed the contest of ideas, would surely have cringed at this asinine remark. For all its strengths, the Coalition was now weakened by reneging one of its foundation assets: its acceptance of many voices within one team. Ministers spoke as men – and they were mostly men – who feared any display of humanity would see them torn down as weaklings. No one dared be Malcolm Fraser. Or Malcolm Turnbull.

Long before Fraser, there was a wily Liberal scheme that I have sometimes thought might be the progenitor of the ferociously inventive Migration Excision Zone devised by John Howard's lawyers. Paul Hasluck, Minister for Territories through the 1950s, combated a Northern Territory court decision to throw the celebrated Aboriginal artist Albert Namatjira in prison on liquor charges in a most clever way: he gazetted a huge tract of bush west of Alice Springs as a "prison," so that Namatjira could wander free on his lands. In these times, that would be called "racist." Probably, it was racist. It was also the right thing to do.

I had learned that dead children demanded an Indonesian Solution – maybe even in combination with a Malaysian one, should that country ever truly democratise. I wished I had the faith to believe that Nyai Roro Kadul, Queen of the Southern Sea, had taken the children to her care. Their parents, too.

News finally came of Hasti. Fars News out of Iran ran an interview with her father, identified as Amir Ali Shirali Esmaeili. It was a Q & A and began with his denying rumours he was a drug user. He said he did not know that Hasti had been heading to Australia with Fatemah, his ex-wife. He rejected claims he did not work hard to get his daughter back. "It's a lie," he said, saying he went to Iran's foreign ministry on the day he heard Fatemah died and booked a ticket for Indonesia, but the man who was caring for Hasti in Jakarta advised him not to come. The story was strange. The father said he had been speaking to Hasti every day by phone while she was in Jakarta, but when she arrived back in Tehran the UNHCR had handed her straight to an Iranian government welfare organisation. The father was not allowed to see her.

> Journalist: We heard you use drugs and they won't allow Hasti to live with you. Is that right?
>
> Father: No, it's a lie. If I use drugs, why they don't catch me now?
>
> Fatemah's family are saying that to news agencies.
>
> Journalist: Does Hasti know that Fatemah is dead?
>
> Father: Yes. After three weeks a psychiatrist told her. [It was more like two months.]
>
> Journalist: You remarried after being divorced to Fatemah?
>
> Father: Yes. But my new wife love Hasti. And I love her also.

Mitt, after his sinking experience, had weighed his options and decided to register with the UNHCR and wait it out, as long as it took, for resettlement. My sincere hope was that he would one day find his way to Australia as a refugee. He was a good person. He was also wealthy, and Iranian. I heard from Reza, my Afghan friend, that New Zealand was a nice place, after all.

He still wanted to get to Australia.

25 February 2014

Paul Toohey travelled throughout the region reporting on asylum seekers as a senior journalist for News Corp Australia.

FOUND IN TRANSLATION

Correspondence

Rowan Callick

If you are a member of any of Australia's elites, you might be forgiven for wondering why Linda Jaivin needs to write, or Black Inc. to publish, an essay subtitled "In praise of a plural world." Surely that goes without saying? Who doesn't want to be able to eat paella and sushi as well as pies and snags?

Australians often congratulate ourselves on our form of multiculturalism. But it doesn't always reach even first base. After writing a piece in January lamenting the absence of Asia from the books-or-films-of-the-year lists for 2013, or from the claimed holiday reading piles of Australian leaders – who seem to remain fixated on the ubiquitously marketed products of the Old World, of London or New York – I received a sobering message on my office answerphone. The reader – who sounded educated, with a polysyllabic vocabulary – branded me a member of the "traitor class," describing Asians and especially Chinese as "the lowest forms of humanity."

So, point made. The case presented by Jaivin does still need to be argued. And not only to people like my anonymous caller. Most of Australia's elite is lost even before translation. Ours remains, really, a pretty narrow world – surprisingly so, given the extent of the excitement and the opportunities that await us not so far away. Those of us who engage with the countries and cultures of our region beyond tourism – doing business, writing, whatever – are such a slender squad that we tend to know each other, as if we're all collectors of a particular type of stamp or spotters of a specially intriguing train.

Hence the enjoyment with which I read Jaivin's essay. It's not exactly systematic but, hey, who cares when her anecdotes are so good?

I was especially drawn to her story about musician Billy Bragg, who like me grew up in deeply unfashionable Essex, east of London. He exhibited, in Beijing back in 1989, the monumental lack of empathy to parade his "socialist" credentials to a bunch of bohemian young Chinese. No wonder that after a brief silence, Chinese politeness overcame embarrassment to produce the most appropriate response: "So ... what kind of amp do you use...?"

When I was at school, I used to write to embassies in London asking them to send any free information about their countries. The more exotic to me, the better. The arrival of the post was a frequent cause of excitement. Wow, so this is what a Bulgarian communal farm looks like, or a Mexican fiesta. The first time I set foot in Asia was stepping off the ferry across the Bosphorus from European Istanbul. What a thrill.

Mike Smith, the ANZ chief executive driving the bank's thrust into Asia, described to me his arrival at Hong Kong's former airport, Kai Tak, where you could once look into apartments from the plane as you approached to land. When he emerged from the airport, he said, he looked around at the lights, he smelt the Cantonese smells, and he thought: "This ... is it."

That's the first step towards translation, your "This is it" moment. Without it, you're just obliging your employer, taking a brief break from the "real world" back home or responding to a white paper.

The next step is to start to learn about the new place's history and culture, and its language; they're all wrapped up together. You may not become fluent in, say, Mandarin or Bahasa Indonesia, but if you're going to spend time there or with people from there, you need to put in some effort.

My first real go, after French and the very helpful classical languages – Latin and Ancient Greek – at school, was with Tok Pisin, the Papua New Guinea lingua franca. This is a real language, with its own grammar and core Melanesian vocabulary, not a bastardisation of English, and I learnt then that however sophisticated and multilingual people are, their home language, the language of the heart, is what they – we – tend to use when emotions are to the fore, from grief to humour to anger to love.

I also learnt from surveying people's faces – whether blank, puzzled or wounded – that sarcasm, especially, is a tool that is both useless and ugly when used in conversation with people in their second language. It came as second nature, a favourite humorous device demonstrating knowingness as I grew up in England. But in the bin it had to go. I had to change, to lose a little of myself, if I weren't to be lost altogether in translation.

Heroes of mine step off most pages of Jaivin's essay, headed by Simon Leys and including the likes of Liu Xiaobo and Ingmar Bergman. And Murakami. Even though, while in Japan recently, I was told by an interpreter that her own appetite for the iconic baby-boomer writer was diminished when she heard him argue bull-headedly about a piece of translation of his own, into Japanese. He insisted that when a writer uses the second person in English, this always means they are addressing a specific person or persons. My acquaintance rightly pointed out that formulations as in recipes ("then you add a pinch of paprika") are often impersonal.

When you make the effort to translate, to understand, you might be temporarily confused. For instance, the Chinese characters for "hand" and "paper" are about the same as the relevant Japanese kanji characters, but they are pronounced quite differently, and in combination mean "envelope" in Japanese but "toilet paper" in Chinese.

But you are unlikely to be lost. When you take a step towards others, they will usually reciprocate.

If you don't even ask, misunderstandings multiply or deepen. I once worked with a Japanese designer whose uncle came on a visit to Melbourne, his first overseas trip. How did Uncle enjoy himself? we asked on our colleague's return from seeing his uncle off. All went extremely well, except that Uncle expressed sadness for all the young women forced to work as prostitutes in the city. He had spent the last few days pondering about those he saw hanging around outside office towers, and come to the only conclusion that made sense to him. His nephew had to explain, eventually, that smoking is banned in Australian office blocks ...

I was taken to dinner a few years ago, when I was living in Beijing, by my Australian translator friends Jane Pan and Martin Merz, with a bunch of translators who get together regularly to swap notes about the biz. Naturally, everyone was curious about who had been commissioned to do what, for how big a fee. It was a tumultuous session, more like the Biblical Tower of Babel referred to by Jaivin than to an academic library. But like others who, in however modest a way, seek to understand and explain people to each other, they seemed to have found something in translation: the core human value of empathy.

Rowan Callick

FOUND IN TRANSLATION

Correspondence

Brian Nelson

Linda Jaivin, in her rich and wide-ranging essay, makes a compelling case for the importance of translation as the "invisible skein" that binds today's "plural world"; and she makes her case in a splendidly entertaining manner.

Despite the obvious benefits of speaking and reading more than one language in a globalised world, and the fact that translation, by its very nature, is transnational, translation still elicits widespread distrust or simple disregard; and English remains resistant to translations: a mere 3 per cent of books published in English are translations. Recognition of translation as a cultural necessity cannot be separated from appreciation of the skills associated with the practice of translation, especially literary translation. People sometimes think of translation as an essentially mechanical activity, as a kind of degraded substitute for the work translated, or as a kind of subservience, in which translators subjugate their own creativity to the demands of the original text. They wouldn't think that way about an actor or a musician, so if they can appreciate the dimension of *performance* in relation to music or theatre, why not in relation to translation?

The answer lies partly in the translator's investment, so to speak, in his invisibility. As Simon Leys has written:

> The paradox which the translator encounters while obstinately pursuing his harrowing task inheres in the fact that he is not setting about erecting a monument to commemorate his talent, but on the contrary is endeavouring to efface all trace of his own existence. The translator is spotted only when he has failed; his success lies in ensuring he be forgotten. The search for the natural and proper expression is the search for that which *no longer feels like a translation.* What is required is to give to the reader the illusion that he has direct access to the original. The ideal translator is an invisible man.

Nevertheless, translators need to be protected from this paradox. The nature of literary translation as an intrinsically creative activity needs to be recognised. Translation is a peculiarly intense form of reading; and it is a form of creative writing, involving a multiplicity of exact choices about voice, register, rhythm, syntax, sounds, connotations, denotations, the colour and texture of words – all those factors that make up "style" and reflect the marriage between style and semantic content. Style is vision. If you don't get the style, you miss the vision. The activity of the writer and that of the translator are indivisible.

The more translators are treated as creative writers, or rewriters, the more translations, better translators and a richer literary culture we'll have. Susan Sontag was right to remind us, in a 2003 essay, that translation is "the circulatory system of the world's literatures." Space needs to be created in the global language that is English for multiple voices, for voices from all over the world. Government can help to create that space by providing the type of support translation enjoys in Europe, where many countries have extensive programs run by government agencies and government-sponsored foundations to facilitate the global dissemination of domestic literature and to ensure that works written in other languages are brought into their language. An Australian Centre for Literary Translation would be a great thing.

The central theme of Jaivin's essay is the nexus between language and culture. Her essay, taken as a whole, offers a fine rebuttal of the remarkably crass suggestion by Lawrence Summers, former president of Harvard University and a key economic adviser to President Obama during his first term, that, given the emergence of English as a global language and the rapid progress in machine translation, investment in foreign-language learning has diminishing returns. Even if we consider this proposition purely in terms of economic advantage, it is not convincing.

But the main objection to Summers' statement (leaving aside the red herring about machine translation) notes the cultural parochialism it appears to embody. Jaivin rightly stresses the importance of foreign-language learning as "the breeding ground of translators and translation"; more broadly, she stresses the cultural richness derived from diversity: "civilisation is ... that process by which cultures open themselves up to others, confront the challenges they offer, and develop." This is a (somewhat familiar) historical fact as well as a feature of the contemporary world. The great texts of Western civilisation were transmitted through translation. As Milan Kundera has written: "Common European thought is the fruit of the immense toil of translators. Without translators, Europe would not exist..." Culture is embedded in language. Really knowing a culture – a particular vision of life, particular ways of thinking and behaving – means knowing it from the inside, through its language. Access to other cultures, and the rich variety of the world's cultures, will slowly be lost if the learning of foreign languages is downgraded. As Lydia Davis has commented, "if we know no other languages but our own we are terribly isolated and impoverished." Jaivin notes that only 12 per cent of Year 12 students in Australia today study a foreign language. That figure is dismayingly, desperately and unnecessarily low.

Brian Nelson

FOUND IN TRANSLATION

Correspondence

Julie Rose

Found in Translation is elegant and engaging, of course; it's also instructive, even to a full-time translator like me.

Anything that makes translation, and translators, visible is good for all of us, general public included; but you know translation has finally hit the cultural radar when a writer-translator of Jaivin's gifts can follow David Marr's polemic on George Pell and the Church's handling of priestly paedophilia with a polemic on the burning issue of translation, for an avid non-specialist Quarterly Essay readership, which also manages to feel urgent.

Translators have been talking translation for some time now, and Jaivin's essay is a useful synthesis of what some of them have been saying; but they've largely been talking to each other. It's nice when a broader audience is addressed – proof, I hope, that we've come a long way from the days when talk of translation could clear a room, so to speak, faster than a poetry reading – even for a specialist audience. In this country, a lot of people have worked hard to make this so, from individuals to bodies like PEN, the

Australian Association for Literary Translation and the NSW Community Relations Commission to sundry arts organisations, and a number of university language departments, which offer avenues for fostering, exploring and supporting translation. There are specialised courses now, and degrees and even the vague promise of "careers" (in the old days, people fell into the job, often on their travels, simply as literate, language-proficient scholars open to the world). A swag of world-class local translators have been rewarded with prizes, the NSW Premier's Translation Prize now being among the most generous in the world.

But Jaivin's essay is also *necessary,* given the dire turn that language-learning in Australia has taken, as she outlines, and the drying-up of funding for translation, as well as the enduring lack of interest in translation in the print media here, where even high-profile literary translations are often, still, ignored altogether or not reviewed as translations (are we really stuck with a monolingual body of reviewers?).

As Jaivin makes clear, we've still got a way to go, all over the Anglophone world in particular, before we Ariadnes of the cross-cultural labyrinth are more than vaguely visible to the public eye, or, better yet, the focus centres on the ball of thread. The status of that ball of thread as independent artefact is far from assured, even within the translation world itself, as is clear from the occasionally rancorous ongoing debates that Jaivin touches on in her nice round-up of the issues. Such debates centre on definitions of "faithfulness" and "authenticity" and the degree to which a translation, particularly a literary translation, should or can follow the original; and even the degree to which any translation succeeds *on its own terms.*

As recently as 2013, Roland Kelts, a contributing editor to an American literary magazine featuring new Japanese work in translation, questioned the very point of translation in the *New Yorker:* "I can't help but wonder if the translation of literature, where the strengths and even personality of the original are embedded in the language, is futile, however heroic." *Futile ...* All those fabulous contributions to world literature, our transcultural heritage?

Jaivin's essay speaks eloquently against such a defeatist ethic. Her vision is all-inclusive: the humble interpreter, even the "document drone," at last find a home. Jaivin's first major revelation: it's *all* translation. Her second: it's *all* political.

But Jaivin's attitude is nuanced and without hubris. I think that's what I like most about her essay: its relaxed and easy spaciousness. Free of defensiveness, Jaivin is able to cheerfully accommodate all possibilities along the spectrum, from what is found and even gained in translation, to what may well be lost, or at least a little fudged, or even trashed or subverted. She can calmly debunk a host of myths, like the myth of transparency, at last pointing out that translation is not a pane of glass you look through at the original

– it is the glass you look at; and that "glass" is the translator's work, both as an independent creation *and* as an interpretation of the original.

We seem to have a lot of trouble with that notion, no doubt because of translation's unique intellectual-property status. Translation, all translation, depends, at least initially, on the prior existence of something else – the writer's intellectual property, in the case of literature. To some, this smacks of a "wilful passing off" of the kind the law defines as plagiarism and copyright infringement. The paradox is that translators *are meant to be copying* the writer's text, and are often castigated when they're felt to deviate from it; yet there is no way they cannot deviate from it: French grammar is not English grammar; a Mandarin word may simply not exist in English, or German.

As William Weaver, the translator of modern Italian classics, once said, "the original is only the starting point." (Weaver, who died recently at the age of seventy-nine, was a man from the heroic age of translation, when a translator of calibre could grow rich introducing a writer of calibre to a new audience.) Every word you, who need the translation, read will be one that the translator, who doesn't need it, writes. As Murakami's American translator, Jay Rubin, points out, when you read his translations of Murakami, you are reading *him,* Jay Rubin, even if Murakami isn't entirely happy with that fact. Jaivin would say, more subtly: Murakami *and* Jay Rubin. I'd add Jay Rubin *as* Murakami, not as Jay Rubin. Translation is not an exact "copy," but it *is* a "speaking likeness" – an imitation of the writer's style. We think of style as inimitably particular, yet the whole brief is to imitate, in a completely different language, the *style* of the original, accurately capturing, without overriding, the author. Yet every word of this reinvention will be the translator's, and coloured by the translator's personality and cultural range. "The original is faithful to the translation" (Jorge Luis Borges): Murakami as Jay Rubin?

We understand, with Jaivin, that this circularity is the pleasure principle at work, but that it only works with scrupulous precision and skill. You take out what you bring to the task of translation, as producers and consumers ... which is why we need to engage with translation with more depth and less narrowness. When done with creative élan, it is a twin kindness: to the original writer and to the new audience.

Julie Rose

FOUND IN TRANSLATION

Correspondence

John Minford

Linda Jaivin is as entertaining and effervescent as ever. In her essay she says a great deal about translation, some of it personal and anecdotal, some conceptual and reflective. She points enthusiastically to the extraordinary opportunities that exist in this theoretically multicultural and polyglot country for the serious study and practice of the art of translation. My own perspective is somewhat bleaker. I had the privilege and pleasure of attending one such extraordinary opportunity, late in 2010, when Nicholas Jose and friends assembled a wonderful symposium on translation in Sydney. It was indeed a splendid and exciting occasion. But how can we ever hope to convey the splendour, and the excitement of the "lifeblood" activity that is literary translation – based as it must be on the careful study of language and literature – to the managerial bureaucrats who now run this country's universities, suspicious as they are of both languages and literature per se, let alone literary translation? The steady decline in the study of "letters" is a symptom of the universities' failure to foster civilisation – what the Chinese call *wenming,* so well paraphrased by Jaivin as that "brightening and clarification that come with intellectual engagement with language and literature." The failure is a worldwide malaise, but the local strain seems particularly virulent.

When I returned to the Australian National University in 2006, among the first meetings I attended was one held to discuss proposed changes to the undergraduate curriculum in Asian studies. Buried halfway through a long document was a paragraph in which the faculty announced its intention to do away with "literature" altogether as a "cognitive elective," making room for more trendy options such as gender and security studies. I raised my hand and protested that "letters" had surely always been at the heart of a university education. Were my colleagues really happy to sit by and watch their passing without so much as a murmur? To my surprise, one by one other hands went up in support of my objection and we managed to postpone indefinitely this "execution by neglect."

During subsequent months I came face to face with the attitude that lay behind this dark moment. I proposed to teach old-fashioned introductory courses on Chinese literature – poetry, fiction, drama – and a seminar on the translation of Chinese literature in general, and when I let this be known, a number of concerned and no doubt well-intentioned colleagues advised me instead to put forward course proposals with titles such as "Concepts of masculinity in eighteenth-century Chinese fiction" or 'Transgender practices in Chinese traditional theatre.' This, I was informed, would be more in keeping with current university trends, and was moreover what students themselves wanted

I subsequently found my students to be thoroughly delighted by the experience of reading Chinese fiction and poetry in translation, unadorned and without the slightest filter of postmodern, post-colonialist, feminist or other theory. It was for them a refreshing exploration of a new world, and often I caught them "looking at each other with a wild surmise," like Keats after he had dipped into Homer in Chapman's version.

I suppose that by their very nature, translators of literature have tended to be guardians of tradition. A century ago, Chinese intellectuals embarked upon a wholesale rejection of their own tradition in favour of modernity, science and democracy – an enterprise later referred to as the May Fourth Movement (it included the discarding of the literary mode of expression known as Classical Chinese). Two of the most outspoken critics of this New Culture Movement were the widely admired translators Lin Shu and Yan Fu, both of whom had used Classical Chinese when introducing to China the masterpieces of Western literature and thought. Lin Shu wrote a famous letter in which he predicted that with the dismantling of the classical literary framework that had sustained centuries of "civilisation," the next Chinese generation would become virtually illiterate.

Over the subsequent century, cultural vandalism became the norm, especially after the establishment of the People's Republic. In 1966 Fou Lei, the prolific translator of Balzac, Romain Rolland and Voltaire among others, and incidentally, the father of the pianist Fou Ts'ong, tragically chose, together with his wife, to commit suicide during the first devastating weeks of the Great Proletarian Cultural Revolution, having endured the hysterical denunciations of the Red Guards and the brutal ransacking of his home in Shanghai. Fou Lei's greatness as a translator was due not only to his fluent knowledge of French and English but also (and perhaps more importantly) to his wide reading in traditional Chinese literature and his deep immersion in Chinese thought and aesthetics. He was a wen-ren, a literatus, in the old Chinese sense, someone who revered the written word, who could not bear to see his language and culture being butchered as it was by the regime, his ideals trampled on. With his untimely death, China probably lost its one chance of having a decent version of Proust. Barbarism prevailed again.

Translation is likely to flourish in a humane, literate and articulate society. When E.V. Rieu (himself a translator) founded the Penguin Classics in 1944, in wartime London, he was able to call upon the talents of a remarkable stable of writer-translators, which included Robert Graves, Dorothy Sayers and J.M. Cohen. After Rieu's death in 1964, Betty Radice and Robert Baldick (both fine translators) continued this tradition. In 1970 Betty commissioned among many other titles a complete five-volume version of the great Chinese novel The Story of the Stone – long before the world's publishers were falling over themselves to include things Chinese in their lists. This commission was the result of a recommendation from Betty's friend Arthur Cooper, a literatus of the old school who worked in intelligence and happened to know Chinese (and translate Chinese poetry).

***

When I was a schoolboy we had to learn by heart Keats's famous sonnet "On first looking into Chapman's Homer." It was never made sufficiently clear to us at the time that the poem was really an Ode in Praise of Translation. It was thanks to Chapman the Elizabethan translator that Keats felt "like some watcher of the skies when a new planet swims into his ken." Such is the magic of the translated word. Such is its power to open minds and create civilisation.

Alberto Manguel ends the chapter of his A *History of Reading* entitled "The Translator as Reader" with these memorable words, which could serve as a challenge and inspiration for all of us engaged in the teaching of literature, language and translation: "Translation may be an impossibility, a betrayal, a fraud, an invention, a hopeful lie – but in the process, it makes the reader a wiser, better listener; less certain, far more sensitive, *seliglicher* [more soulful, and therefore, argues Manguel, blessed]." This is surely a noble aspiration, and one to which we should be fiercely loyal, in the face of the Nothing that is engulfing us all.

John Minford

FOUND IN TRANSLATION

Response to Correspondence

Linda Jaivin

I laughed aloud when I read Julie Rose's comment that the publication of *Found in Translation* in this forum is "proof ... that we've come a long way from the days when talk of translation could clear a room, so to speak, faster than a poetry reading." The social currency of translation, in Australia at least, has for many years been only marginally higher than actuarial science. To say you're a translator prompts the question, "From what language?" but then what ideally could create a conversational roundabout often leads straight into the following dead-ends: "I'm not good at languages." "My cousin studied Mandarin." "The Chinese aren't as friendly as Thais." And my favourite, said to me many years ago by a Greek diplomat in London: "So you are not just a pretty face."

Both Rose and Brian Nelson, in their generous and collegial comments, have homed in on the subject of the translator's invisibility, which is paradoxically a matter of some pride and little joy for literary translators. When Olivier (or Toby Schmitz, to translate the example to Australia) plays Hamlet, you want to believe you are watching Hamlet, but at the end of the play it's Olivier or Schmitz who gets to stand on stage and bask in the applause. The literary translator, by contrast, sits at home hopefully, possibly morosely scanning the reviews and waiting for someone to say something, anything, about her work, though preferably not just that the translation is "fluent." Yet, as Nelson writes, "The nature of literary translation as an intrinsically creative activity needs to be recognised" – especially if we are to have "more translations, better translators and a richer literary culture." As a Sydney-sider I was delighted to learn from Rose's remarks that the NSW Premier's Translation Prize is the most generous in the world – especially as she won it in 2003.

She and Nelson both affirm the importance of institutional support for translation. Nelson makes what I think is a suggestion well worth considering: the establishment of an Australian Centre for Literary Translation. Of course, as Rose points out, "in the old days, people fell into the job, often on their travels, simply as literate, language-proficient scholars open to the world." That certainly describes how I became a translator. There was no grand plan, just a delight in my new language and the cultural encounters and experiences that it opened up to me, and a desire to play with it as much as possible. I wasn't thinking about skeins or global cultural trade imbalances – I was having a particularly stimulating kind of fun.

A similar open-minded curiosity about what this great big plural world has to offer drove a young Rowan Callick to write to embassies asking for free information on their countries. "The arrival of the post was a frequent cause of excitement. Wow, so this is what a Bulgarian communal farm looks like, or a Mexican fiesta." It's a charming anecdote, and a fitting prelude to his life of travel, language study (French, Latin, Greek and Papua New Guinea's lingua franca of Tok Pisin, just for starters) and, of course, a career in journalism, another métier into which many of us simply "fell."

Callick's observation about how the combination of the Chinese characters for "hand" and "paper" mean "toilet paper" in Chinese but "envelope" in Japanese reminded me of one of my own first, ill-fated attempts to translate my knowledge of Chinese into useful information for getting around Japan. Travelling alone and on my first visit there, I was looking for someplace to eat a simple meal when I spotted a sign with the Chinese character for soup. I didn't realise until I walked inside what exactly would be in the soup – people. It was a public bathhouse. The Japanese use of the character had shifted the original sense of hot water in a rather different direction.

I appreciate the point Callick makes, too, about how sarcasm, normal in the context of the banter between native speakers of English becomes "a tool that is both useless and ugly when used in conversation with people in their second language." To put it another way, it is one of those culturally specific habits that can take the wheels off a conversation in a vehicular language. He comments how he had to "change, to lose a little of myself, if I weren't to be lost altogether in translation."

There is one point in Callick's response where it occurs to me that we may in fact be a bit lost to one another in translation. He interprets my story about Billy Bragg explaining his socialist beliefs to mystified young Beijing rockers in 1989 (the year of the Tiananmen pro-democracy protests) as demonstrating how Bragg exhibited "a monumental lack of empathy." I blame myself for not adequately contextualising the anecdote. For one thing, the rockers had heard that Bragg was a socialist and were genuinely curious about why. But the vision of a kinder-hearted, social justice–based vision of socialism that he elaborated was so far from their experience of state socialism as interpreted by the Communist Party of China that they could barely understand it as socialism at all. Challenged further by the laborious process of exposition – in which Bragg spoke, I translated, and then he spoke again – they eventually dropped away into puzzlement and then something like boredom. But they were never hostile or contemptuous towards him, and at the meal we had afterwards, and the gig we attended after that, they showed him nothing but warmth and respect.

I should also add that the meeting occurred on Saturday, 15 April 1989, the very day that the reformist former Communist Party secretary-general Hu Yaobang died. The news did not interest the musos all that much; I recall someone making off-colour jokes based on the rumour that Hu had died of a heart attack while on the toilet. Then the conversation moved on. None of us, foreign or Chinese, was aware that around the same time, students on campuses around Beijing were conducting impassioned and idealistic discussions about the kinder-hearted version of socialism that they believed might have been possible had Hu not been pushed aside.

The following Monday, Bragg and I ascended the rostrum of Tiananmen, taking photos of each other in our best Mao poses, when he spotted a small knot of people around the Monument to the People's Heroes in the centre of the square. He asked me what was going on there, and, as I wrote in *The Monkey and the Dragon,* I shrugged: "No idea." Sharp China specialist that I was, I had no idea that we were watching the very beginnings of the pro-democracy protests that within two weeks would sweep the city.

For a while, Bragg and I tried to get up a documentary on Chinese rock 'n' roll with him as presenter. We even planned to re-stage that scene with the rockers and the question about the amps for the film. He has, I can assure Callick, a very good sense of humour.

John Minford is one of *the* great translators from Chinese and I truly appreciate his sober words on the state of the arts and education – and am deeply moved that he found the time to write his response despite having recently been seriously ill. I too am a passionate believer in the intrinsic value of the study of literature, of "letters" and language. Although not of the academy I have enough of a close association with it, through visiting fellowships at the Australian National University and a term chairing the Advisory Board of the School of Arts and Social Sciences at the University of Technology Sydney, to know something of the "malaise" of which he speaks. Administrators and politicians (Christopher Pyne, I'm talking about you) and ideologues of all stripes need to take a few steps back, draw a few deep breaths, and let the liberal arts breathe in return. The tradition of the liberal arts is one that has always allowed and can continue to encourage vibrant and vital debate to flourish, and from which new ideas continue to spring.

A lifelong and ardent feminist (I read *The Female Eunuch* around the age of sixteen, and Betty Friedan's *The Feminine Mystique* before that), I am aware that my thinking about feminism has been richly informed by broad reading in the ancient and modern classics of a number of different cultures. I benefited more from reading (a translation of) *Lysistrata* in a course on Greek plays that told me about the context in which it was written – social values, concerns and obsessions, history and the role of humour in Greek polemics – than I would have, I believe, had I studied it in the context of feminist plays throughout the ages. But that's another issue. I'm open to discussion and even persuasion, so long as those doing the discussing have read widely and deeply enough, in translation or in the original languages, to be persuasive.

Minford concludes with a quotation by Alberto Manguel, whom I had the immense pleasure to meet many years ago when we were both guests of the Melbourne Writers Festival. A creative writer, translator, essayist and anthologist, Manguel remains an inspiration. I feel confident in speaking for all the respondents when I say that, like Minford, I too find in Manguel's words a "noble aspiration" and one worthy of fierce loyalty. The alternative is the ugly, narrow tribalism of Callick's vitriolic caller. Luckily, thanks to thousands of years of translation and the collective energy of translators, the skein that binds us cannot be so easily unravelled.

Linda Jaivin

Rowan Callick is Asia-Pacific editor of the *Australian.* His book *Party Time: Who Runs China and How* was published in 2013.

Linda Jaivin is the author of novels, stories, plays and essays. Her books include *Eat Me,* the China memoir *The Monkey and the Dragon,* and *A Most Immoral Woman.* In 1992 she co-edited the acclaimed anthology of translations *New Ghosts, Old Dreams: Chinese Rebel Voices.* She has done the subtitles for many films, including Chen Kaige's *Farewell My Concubine,* Tian Zhuangzhuang's *Blue Kite,* Zhang Yimou's *Hero* and Wong Kar Wai's *The Grandmaster.* She is a research affiliate in the College of Asia and the Pacific at the ANU and a regular visitor to China.

John Minford is professor of Chinese at the Australian National University. His new translation of the Chinese divination classic, the *I Ching,* will be published later this year.

Brian Nelson is emeritus professor at Monash University and editor of the *Australian Journal of French Studies.* His well-known translations of the novels of Emile Zola include *The Fortune of the Rougons* and *The Ladies' Paradise.* Most recently, he is the coeditor (with Brigid Maher) of *Perspectives on Literature and Translation: Creation, Circulation, Reception.*

Julie Rose is a translator, whose works include the first full original unabridged English translation of Victor Hugo's *Les Misérables* and Alexandre Dumas' *The*

Knight of the Maison-Rouge. In 2003 she was awarded the PEN Translation Prize.

Paul Toohey is chief northern correspondent for the *Australian.* He won a Walkley Award for his first Quarterly Essay, *Last Drinks: The Impact of the Northern Territory Intervention.* He was previously a senior writer at the *Bulletin* and is the author of three books: *God's Little Acre, Rocky Goes West* and *The Killer Within.* He has won the Graham Perkin journalist of the year award and a Walkley award for magazine feature writing. He lives in Darwin.

BACK COVER MATERIAL

Tony Abbott promised to stop the boats. With the help of Kevin Rudd's "PNG solution," he has. But at what cost?

In Quarterly Essay 53, Paul Toohey tells the dramatic stories of asylum seekers heading from Java to Australia, investigates people-smuggling and witnesses the aftermath of a sinking at sea.

Toohey also examines Australian attitudes to boat people, and what politicians have made of these. He assesses the diplomatic fall-out from turning back boats and asks: have we missed our chance for an Indonesian solution, a realistic alternative to the brutally effective system we now have? This is an unflinching look at people at their worst and best – and most ruthless and most vulnerable – by one of Australia's finest reporters.

"Any hope for a genuine regional solution rested with Indonesia, the final stepping stone to Australia ... Why did neither Howard, in his better times with Indonesia, or Labor, from 2007, seek a one-on-one solution with Indonesia? 'The Indonesian Solution.' Those words would have been the most convincing political statement any Australian government could ever deliver to Australian voters on asylum seekers."

Paul Toohey, ***That Sinking Feeling***

Paul Toohey is a senior reporter for News Corp Australia. He won a Walkley Award for his first Quarterly Essay, *Last Drinks: The Impact of the Northern Territory Intervention.* He was previously a senior writer at the *Bulletin* and the *Australian,* has won the Graham Perkin Journalist of the Year Award and is the author of three books: *God's Little Acre*, Rocky Goes West and *The Killer Within.* He lives in Darwin.

QUARTERLY ESSAY presents significant contributions to the general debate. Each issue contains a single essay written at a length of about 25,000 words. It aims to present the widest range of political, intellectual and cultural opinion.

Made in United States
Orlando, FL
04 November 2026

90204434R00098